The Hindu Caste System

Past, Present and Future

Jayaram V

Published by
Pure Life Vision LLC
New Albany, Ohio

The Hindu Caste System: Past, Present, and Future

Copyright © 2025 by Jayaram V. All rights reserved.
Published and Distributed Worldwide by Pure Life Vision LLC., USA.
First edition 2025

No part of this publication may be reproduced, stored in a retrieval system, or transmitted in any form or by any means, electronic, mechanical, photocopying, recording, scanning, or otherwise, now known or hereinafter invented, except for quotations in printed reviews, without the prior written, express permission of the publisher or the author. This strict copyright protection is meant to ensure the respect and integrity of the author's work. Requests to the publisher for permission to print portions of this book or for bulk purchase of the book should be addressed to Pure Life Vision LLC, PO Box 1003, 102 W Main St, New Albany, OH 43054.

NO AI TRAINING: Without in any way limiting the author's and publisher's exclusive rights under copyright, any use of this publication to "train" generative artificial intelligence (AI) technologies to generate text is expressly prohibited. The author reserves all rights to license uses of this work for generative AI training and development of machine learning language models.

Pure Life Vision LLC is a registered company in the U.S.A. Pure Life Vision books and E-Books are available through numerous bookstores, our websites, and our online store. For inquiries, please visit https://www.PureLifeVision.com.

Cover Design © Jayaram V

Library of Congress Publisher Cataloging-in-Publication Data

V, Jayaram, (Vemulapalli)
The Hindu Caste System: Past, Present, and Future
    p. cm
    LCCN: 2025930662
    ISBN- 13: 978-1-935760-18-4
    ISBN -10: 1-935760-18-1
    1. Hinduism. 2. Hinduism--Customs and practices. 3. Hinduism--Religious life. I. Title.

Cover Design by Jayaram V
Printed in the United States of America
10 9 8 7 6 5 4 3 2
First Edition 2025

Contents

Preface 9

Author Notes 11

The Vedic Varna System 15

An Outline of the Four Main Varnas 25

How the Varna System Found Acceptance 32

A Brief History of the Varna System 38

How Tradition Justified Class Distinctions 65

Varna, Dharma, and Varnashrama Dharma 72

The Caste System in Ascetic Traditions 78

The Pros and Cons of the Caste System 83

The Varna As a Way of Life 88

In Defense of the Caste System 95

An Upanishadic Perspective on Varna 102

Reforming the Caste System 106

Footnotes 115

To My Parents, Grandparents, and Teachers

About the Author

Jayaram V is a distinguished author renowned for his unique perspective. With 16 books to his credit, including *Brahman*, *The Awakened Life*, *An Introduction to Hinduism*, *Bhagavadgita: Unveiling the Gita's Secrets*, *Essays on the Bhagavadgita*, *Selected Upanishads*, *Brihadaranyaka and Chandogya Upanishads*, and *Shiva Sutras: Mystic Knowledge Explained*, Jayaram's writings are celebrated globally for their depth and clarity. His works explore themes such as Hinduism, Buddhism, Jainism, Sikhism, Zoroastrianism, spirituality, and self-improvement.

Inspired by the profound knowledge and wisdom contained within these traditions, Jayaram aims to share his insights with others. His academic background in science affords him the objectivity to interpret these subjects with modern insights independent of sectarian biases. Consequently, his writings elegantly bridge the mundane with the mystical and the finite with the infinite.

In 2000, Jayaram founded Hinduwebsite.com to disseminate the ideals of Hinduism, Buddhism, Jainism, Yoga, spirituality, and related topics. Over the past 35 years, he has extensively studied India's religious and spiritual traditions. To learn more about Jayaram V and explore his writings, please visit his websites: Jayaramv.com and Hinduwebsite.com.

Books By Jayaram V

Brahman, Second Edition, 2024

The Bhagavadgita: Unveiling the Gita's Secrets, 2024

The Bhagavadgita: A Simple Translation, Second Edition, 2024

The Awakened Life: Spiritual Knowledge... Second Edition, 2024

Shiva Sutras: Mystic Knowledge Explained, 2024

Brihadaranyaka Upanishad, Revised 2024

Chandogya Upanishad, Revised 2024

Introduction to Hinduism, Revised, 2024

Sadhana Panchakam - The Fivefold Spiritual Practice

Essays on the Bhagavadgita

The Bhagavadgita: A Complete Translation, 2010

Selected Upanishads, 2013

Think Success: Essays on Self-help

Being the Best: Practical Advice for Peace and Happiness

Thoughts and Quotations

The Hindu Caste System, 2025

Preface

This book has been published to create awareness about the Hindu caste system and the need for its reform. Much of the information in this book was written by Jayaram V several years ago and published at Hinduwebsite.com. We decided to compile and publish them as a book. For this publication, Jayaram revisited and improved his earlier work, considering the feedback and developments in the field over the years. We have reorganized his earlier writings into different chapters with appropriate headings, corrections, and improvements. The caste system is a controversial subject. Any views expressed or implied about it are bound to attract contrasting opinions and comments from the diverse sections of the community according to their beliefs, worldviews, and conditioning. Caste is deeply embedded and internalized in the minds of Hindus. From an early age, it becomes an integral part of their mindsets and influences their thinking. For centuries, it has been a critical factor in the social and cultural affairs of Hindus. We cannot live in denial of it or gloss over it, nor can we accept it in today's value system as the defining aspect of our conduct and social or personal relationships. We are confident that this book of Jayaram offers a broad and balanced view of the Hindu caste system, its history, current status, impact on the community and the future of Hinduism, and whether it can be reformed to fit it into the present-day value system. We request you to read it with tolerance, understanding, and compassion for those who have been living in the shadows for centuries due to caste inequalities and discrimination.

Publishers
Jan 21, 2025

Please note: The explanatory notes for the annotations are at the end of the book.

Author Notes

I belong to a well-educated Hindu family and was born in combined Andhra Pradesh a decade after India's independence. I grew up and lived in Eastern, Northern, Central, and Southern India and imbibed the local cultures. I also lived in Mumbai for almost a year. My education happened in Andhra Pradesh, but until my schooling began and later, I spent considerable time with my parents in Central India, where my father worked, and my parents lived for much of their lives. I spent much of my teen years in college hostels. Later, after I got my job, I lived in different parts of India due to my job responsibilities. Subsequently, I lived in Nigeria for five years and, from there, moved to the US, where I have been living now for the last 25 years.

In these years, life taught me many lessons and helped me develop a broader view of people and relationships. I also learned about multiple cultures. My parents told me I used to speak in Odiya, too, but I do not remember anything about it. My maternal grandfather, in whose care I grew up and spent much of my school days, was well-educated and disciplined with a strong moral sense of right and wrong. He graduated with a graduate degree in Bachelor of Arts from a college in the erstwhile Madras Province, during the First World War and served under British rule as a police officer. I have imbibed many good things from him, including discipline and the determination to complete what I start. He encouraged me to excel in my studies and inculcated in me many good habits and a passion for reading and learning from early childhood. All my relations in those days, including my mother, aunts, grandmother, and mother, were educated and had a basic knowledge of the world at a time when the literacy rate in India was very low, and people lived and died mostly in the villages where they were born.

I have written about my family background (which I usually avoid out of modesty and keep myself incognito) because I do not want readers to mistakenly think that my views about the Hindu caste system are born out of some personal prejudice or deep-seated resentment. I have no personal stake in writing about this topic. Indeed, it pains me to think about it since topics such as this bring out a lot of negative energy. I have lived a good life and enjoyed the privileges that came with my family's upper caste background. Until I grew up, I never gave any importance to my caste identity since it was never an issue for me. The universe has been kind to me by putting me in favorable circumstances and giving me a decent start in life, for which I am forever grateful.

However, as a child, I saw social and economic disparities. I saw how people lived in different parts of each village according to their social and economic status. The most important ones lived in the prime areas, and the lesser ones in the periphery. Now, I see that it was also related to castes and their relative importance in society. Castes obviously played an important role in determining the social and economic status of people and how they lived or were treated. As I look back, I can see how the caste system was at work in schools and college campuses. Even the faculties were drawn into its ambit. Some favored students from their castes and liberally graded them while discriminating against others and dealing with the discrimination of other faculty members. In some villages, I saw caste conflicts often leading to violent hostilities and group clashes.

Therefore, I believe that I have firsthand knowledge of how the Indian caste system works at the grassroots level in the real world to write about it with some authority. Castes are an important part of India's social system and group dynamics. They influence people's behavior, relationships, political alignment, and career prospects. Caste discrimination is acute in rural areas where remnants of the old feudal system still exist, and some people genuinely believe in their social superiority and their God-given right to indulge in it.

Despite its problems and disadvantages, the caste system is most likely here to stay for a long time because it is also a powerful cultural factor and almost inseparable from Hinduism. For various reasons, which I have discussed in one of the chapters, it is also not entirely bad. It surely has some redeeming features. For example, it imparts group identities to people, fosters relationships and group cohesion among people of the same caste, and helps them experience unity, fraternity, security, strength, and belongingness. It is not uncommon to see in various parts of India people of the same caste or social strata helping and supporting each other in difficulties. It also often helps people unite under a common banner and negotiate with government authorities or politicians from a position of strength for social and economic benefits.

In these circumstances, the best anyone can do is to minimize its adverse effects and accommodate its positive features without exploiting it or creating divisions and conflicts. The growing influence of cities and city culture is a redeeming feature since, in the cities, amidst a sea of people, castes and social status become irrelevant and do not draw as much attention or importance as they do in small places. People do not have much time to think about them as they have to deal with more serious issues about their survival and success. Further, as the mind expands due to increasing social interactions and personal relationships, one begins to see people as people, not as members of some caste or community.

Although the status of the many castes has improved, there are still many villages and communities in India where people from lower castes are ill-treated or barred from entering public and religious places. In some places, they are not allowed to draw drinking water from the wells used by the upper castes. Such practices do not augur well for the future of Hinduism. They create a sense of inferiority, insecurity, and dependence in people who are subjected to them and lead to disunity, divisions, and social tensions. Intercaste marriages, especially between higher and lower-caste Hindus, are hugely unpopular. Indeed, they are more unpopular than interfaith marriages and often result in honor killings, as displeased elders see that as a challenge to their reputation and social status and retaliate to repair the situation. In many villages and perhaps towns, lower caste people cannot freely buy property where higher caste people live, even if they have money. They face a similar problem in renting or leasing properties. Caste conflicts and discrimination exist at various levels, overtly and covertly. They reinforce and perpetuate age-old beliefs, prejudices, inequalities, and injustices and keep the community divided and vulnerable to outside influences.

At the same time, we cannot ignore the positive side of the caste system. It played an important role in the preservation and continuation of Hinduism through numerous challenges and political upheavals. It also helped people find solace and comfort in each other as they faced common problems particular to their groups or castes. Keeping this in mind, I tried to approach the subject from a broader perspective and present a balanced view. We know that it is an inherited problem, that everyone is stuck in it, and no one, in particular, is responsible for it. Almost every caste and community has been adapting to the current reality and waking up to the fact that it needs a permanent solution in the larger interests of all. If Hindus work collectively, they can keep the caste system for the good of all, removing all the ills for which it is known.

Some statements and observations in this book may sound critical to some readers, especially if they have been victims of caste prejudices or still believe in their privileged birth. Everyone is different and may have different perspectives on the same issues, depending on their experiences and perceptions. Therefore, I do not expect everyone to appreciate them. When I wrote about the caste system some twenty years ago, the Internet was in its early phases; the world was inclined to accept opposing views, Google did not have the kind of dominance it has now; speech-policing and safe spaces were never heard of, and people were not troubled as much by the words and labels they found ideologically upsetting on the Internet. Today, this is not the case. Writers who dare to express their unfiltered opinions about sensitive topics are vulnerable to unfiltered criticism and hurtful comments on social media. It is a risk every writer has to take. Indeed, sometimes, it is necessary to speak the truth and face the reality for the common good. Therefore, please read this book with tolerance, understanding, and the awareness that everyone on this planet deserves to live with dignity and respect and pursue excellence or whatever they value and cherish.

The Vedic Varna System

Special Note*: Although the words caste and Varna are used synonymously by many, the ancient Varna system is distinct from the modern caste system. Sometimes, it is necessary to keep the distinction between the two for clarity and understanding. Therefore, I used them differently in some cases and synonymously in some, according to the context. I also used class, group, or social division to refer to them. I hope readers will note this while reading.*

Varna literally means color, hue, or complexion. It has other meanings, such as a class of men, tribe, race, species, a word or syllable, outward appearance, form, figure, a cloak or mantle, and the arrangement of the subject in a song. In other words, Varna primarily refers to the physical appearance of things or beings and their categorization based on the common characteristics they share within each group or class. Varnakrama refers to the order of such classes or castes. Since Varna also means a letter, varnakrama also means the arrangement of letters in an alphabet. As the name implies, Varna dharma refers to the duties assigned to each class or caste.

Varna in Vedic times

In the early days of its formation, Vedic society had four Varnas, namely Brahmanas, Kshatriyas, Vaishyas, and Shudras. They were not equal in status. Their status is determined by the krama or order assigned to them by tradition, although the Vedas proclaimed them to be created by the same source. Of the four, Brahmanas occupied the highest position as gods upon earth and intermediaries between gods and humans, having unique access to Brahman, the highest of all. Except in certain Vedic rituals, where they had to sit below their kings, which was probably an ancient custom reminiscent of the times when the Kshatriyas occupied the highest position, their position in society was unassailable. Kshatriyas were next to the Brahmanas in the hierarchy. They had the right to claim the divine authority to rule the earth as God's sole representatives and enforce laws as the guardians of Dharma. Vaishyas came later. Their purpose was to create and distribute the wealth necessary to ensure peace and prosperity and achieve the chief aims of human life by promoting Dharma and helping others. The Shudras belonged to the last category. Their obligatory duty was to serve the other three classes in their effort to promote and uphold the Dharma. The first three classes had permission to study and practice the Vedas. The Shudras were barred from even hearing them. Apart from them, there were outcastes (chandalas), the untouchables whose condition was deplorable. They were even barred from entering the localities in each town and village where the higher castes lived.

According to some, the Varna system evolved gradually in Vedic society. First, it seems that there were only three classes, just as there were only three Vedas. All the people who were neither Brahmanas nor Kshatriyas were considered Vaishyas, except the outcastes and outlier groups. This practice seemed to have continued in some parts of India until the end of the Gupta period (600 CE). The Shudra class was probably a latter development, necessitated by the inclusion of many people into the Vedic fold to distinguish the working class from the producing class, as agriculture and cattle rearing became an important part of the Vedic economy and landowning and business communities gained social and political importance. The fourfold Varna system served as insurance for the higher castes, helping them protect and preserve their family occupations, skill development, family lineages, business opportunities, trade, and commerce while precluding many from competing with them.

The system, supported and enforced by scriptural and imperial authority, ensured that each Varna was entrusted with a specific set of obligatory duties (Varna dharmas) called the Dharma of each Varna. These duties were not just tasks to be performed, but they formed the very fabric of the society, ensuring the smooth functioning and balance of the social order. Thus, in Vedic usage, Dharma primarily meant obligatory duty or duties, obligatory in the sense that they must be performed to avoid sinful karma and attain a good birth in the next life. Brahmanas worshipped fire (Agni) and engaged in priestly duties. They studied and taught the Vedas, performed sacrificial rituals for their kings and patrons, observed moral and religious laws enshrined in the scriptures, exemplified virtuous conduct, and worked for the spiritual and temporal welfare of the people they served. Kshatriyas worshipped gods of royalty such as Brahma, Indra, Prajapati, Vayu, Soma, Mitra, and Varuna. They studied the Vedas, trained themselves in martial arts and weaponry, served their kings as the guardians of Dharma and protectors of their kingdoms, fought battles on their behalf, and engaged in religious and spiritual activities for the welfare of all when they were not fighting enemies. Vaishyas worshipped Visvadevas, the gods of commonality. They engaged in trade and commerce, lent money to kings and others when they needed help, trained their children in the professions in which they excelled, performed sacrifices, and gave charity to religious and social causes. Finally, the Shudras worshipped Pusan, the god of the earth, and engaged in obedient service to the other three groups. The law books prescribed severe punishments for those who disobeyed or disrespected the higher castes or violated their prescribed code of conduct.

The historicity of the Varna system

Some historians and scholars tend to either deny the existence of the Varna system or social classes in the Vedic period or gloss over facts, implying that they were invented later by foreigners to denigrate Hinduism. The truth is that we cannot truly doubt the historicity of the Varna system. It has been an integral aspect of Hinduism and India's social, cultural, and anthropological history since the dawn of its unique civilization. It influenced every aspect of life in ancient India. No section of the community was immune to the ripples it created, which still seem to be undulating and creating further ripples. The four Varnas are often equated with races, but this claim is unjustified. No evidence supports that India ever had pure races. Its population has always been as heterogeneous as it is today. The same is true even in the heydays of the Indus Valley Civilization (2500 BCE). It is also incorrect to say that British scholars and historians cleverly invented the caste system to divide and rule India. They might have exploited it or highlighted it using an ancient tradition and nomenclature to their advantage. However, it did clearly exist for a long time before their colonial rule.

The idea or the concept of the Hindu Varna system has a long history and tradition, dating back to the early Vedic period or, perhaps, according to some, even earlier to the Indus Valley times. It is even possible that some form of caste divisions existed outside the Vedic tradition, and the latter adapted it with some modifications to establish a viable social order and preserve their beliefs and practices. The Varnas are clearly and categorically mentioned in the Vedas and other Hindu scriptures, such as the Manusmriti, the Upanishads, and the Bhagavadgita. The caste system was not uniformly implemented or practiced throughout the Indian subcontinent. It prevailed only in the areas ruled by the kings who patronized and practiced the Vedic religion. Elsewhere, barring the outcastes (chandalas), the relationship between the castes varied from region to region, depending upon the power and prestige wielded by each of them, which is the case even today in many parts of rural India.

The Creation Hymn in the Rigveda, which is at least 3000 years old, describes how the four varnas sprang from the different parts of Purusha (Cosmic Person), Brahman's direct manifestation, who contains within Himself universal materiality and consciousness as His fundamental duality. Some historians believe that the Vedic varnas were initially not that rigid but might have become stratified into rigid social divisions in the later period. Probably, the early Varna system accommodated some exceptions and adjustments in its formative period when the Vedic religion was gaining ground. However, it is difficult to accept that the four varnas were merely voluntary groups of people based on their occupations or that people were free to choose their varnas and occupations. The early Vedic society probably consisted of three classes: Brahmanas, Kshatriyas, and Vaishyas. The last group must have consisted of all those who were neither of the first two.

In Vedic times, the varnas carried a lot of importance, especially for people who traced their origin to the ancient lineages and practiced their obligatory duties (Dharma) according to the established traditions and practices as ordained by the Vedas. The social order was characterized by the division of people according to their varnas and the privileges, duties, and responsibilities each of them carried. Going by its name, we may assume that initially, the Varna system was based on skin color rather than professions or occupations. Caste-based occupations and hereditary caste system might have become necessary with the growing diversity of the Indian population and the coming together of many people belonging to diverse social, cultural, and ethnic backgrounds. At least, the grouping and the clearly established divisions helped them perform their respective duties, coexist peacefully, and ensure their collective survival and continuation.

Discrimination, prejudice, and antagonism against particular groups and classes of people based on their race, color, religion, and ethnicity exist even today in many parts of the world despite the existence of laws and constitutional guarantees that explicitly prohibit them and declare them to be punishable offenses. The laws discourage explicit and provable offenses, but they cannot remove the deep-rooted prejudices and discrimination that exist in people's minds as the subterranean muck of centuries-old collective consciousness. In the Vedic times, such prejudices were officially and openly allowed to continue, with the stamp of approval by the dogma and by the people who acted as its designated guardians, upholders, and promulgators. It helped them preserve the purity and integrity of each group and ensure the order and regularity of society. However, as time went on, the purity of each Varna was lost, and the color-based Varna system must have given way to a rigid, hereditary social system in which Dharma or occupational duties became the central factor. This change in people's attitudes is reflected in some Upanishad verses that suggest how one may obtain children of different colors by performing specific rituals.

The fourfold Varna system eventually gave way to a more complex caste system. Castes (kulas) became popular with the emergence of a more diverse social system comprising multiple ethnicities, tribal and linguistic groups, social classes, races, and cultures due to the intermixture of castes, foreign invasions, and the integration of various geographical regions of the Indian subcontinent into large empires and kingdoms ruled by imperial dynasties. Throughout the tumultuous periods of India's history, this new system survived and gained ground in the backdrop of the Varna system, becoming the defining aspect of Hinduism. It influenced even other religions, Buddhism and Jainism in the beginning, and Sikhism and Islam subsequently. Discrimination against the lower varnas existed in ancient India, especially in those communities that practiced the Vedic religion in some form under the tutelage of the rulers and patrons who practiced it and accepted the superiority of Brahmanas and Kshatriyas as a divine injunction. However, we cannot say that it was true with regard to other communities, where other faiths were popular, and rulers and people followed different laws and social norms, customs, and practices.

Varna in the Dharma Shastras

The Varna system was enforced, at least partially, with the help of the Dharma Shastras, the law books that laid down specific guidelines for each group, specifying their respective moral and religious duties and obligations, punishments and atonements for various offenses, laws to regulate marital relationships, the basis of eligibility for inheritance rights, the norms governing women's duties, status, and conduct, etc. Undoubtedly, they were biased and discriminatory in their treatment, approach, and attitude towards the four Varnas, giving preferential treatment to the higher varnas (agra-varnas) and imposing many restrictions upon the lower ones. They favored the upper caste men and were clearly biased against the lower castes and women in general. It can be seen in their proclamations, justifying the superiority of the higher castes, tacit approval of heredity as the basis of a person's caste and caste-related duties, and prescribing differential standards of rewards and punishments for the same offenses committed by the four groups. People's status and inheritance depended upon their heredity, descent, ancestry, and the pedigree of their birth parents. They also limited opportunities for the lower castes to survive and succeed in such a discriminatory system. The survival and continuity of the Shudras, and to some extent Vaishyas, depended upon how well they behaved and aligned with the higher castes and served them.

We must also note that the Dharma Shastras had limited reach. They were not universally enforced in the entire subcontinent since it was divided into numerous kingdoms and hardly ever under one rule or administration. The rulers practiced different faiths and followed different laws to govern their subjects, regulate their conduct, and prescribe punishments for various offenses. The Hindu law books prevailed only when rulers followed them and promulgated them through their officials and provincial rulers. Even then, due to many geographical and physical constraints, it is doubtful how far their authority extended from their capitals. The power to prescribe punishments and resolve disputes was left largely to traditional local committees (panchayats) and village elders. They followed different sets of norms, beliefs, laws, methods, standards, and practices to deliver judgments or prescribe punishments. Even in the areas where Hinduism prevailed, we cannot be sure which laws the rulers and others followed. Hinduism has many law books, and they differ in many respects.

Varnas and castes

Varnas have gone, just as the purity of the color of each Varna, but castes (kulas) are still there as the vestiges of the ancient Varna system. Varna is now used in the sense of caste only. In contemporary Hindu society, you do not hear much about varnas but kulas (castes), which are numerous and vary from region to region. Color is no longer a criterion to distinguish the status of castes, since all castes now consist of people of both dark and fair complexion and cannot be distinguished based purely upon that one factor.

Although the Varna system is outdated and almost defunct in its original sense, it is still there in the background as the social standard since most of the castes tend to identify themselves with one of the original four Varnas. For example, Iyers, Iyyengars, Sharmas, etc., identify themselves with Brahmanas. Land owning Feudal castes such as Kohlis, Khatris, Jats, Gurjars, Reddys, Kammas, Nairs, Chowdhury, Thakurs, etc., whose origin may partly be traced to the intermingling of original varnas and migration of their ancestors, may identify themselves with Kshatriyas or Vaishyas or both. Mittals, Agarwals, Guptas, etc., consider themselves Vaishyas. These claims are difficult to prove since there are no clear historical records to trace their genealogies or origins. Yet, if we have to fit them into the original Varna system, we cannot help making a few compromises. The same problem arises when new people are inducted into Hinduism and assigned a caste identity.

No one clearly knows how so many castes came into existence, from where their ancestors came, and how they gradually settled and gained importance in different parts of India, speaking different languages and specializing in several professions and occupations and arts and crafts. Their affiliation to the original Varnas is based upon tradition or the Gotras (the family lineages) of each group. It is possible that most of them descended from more than one Varna, and some might have used political turmoil and migration to new regions as an opportunity to upgrade themselves with the blessings of the local priestly communities.

Varna in contemporary Hindu society

In today's Hindu society, the varnas and the social order of each Varna or caste (varnakrama) are still important. However, their status and place in the social and economic order varies from region to region. The subject of castes (Varna or kula) and The social order of each Varna or caste (Varna krama) are still sensitive matters in the Hindu community. People may not speak about them openly. Yet, caste divisions and discrimination still exist on a large scale. People, though not all, still give importance to their caste identities and experience a roller coaster of positive and negative emotions depending upon how they perceive themselves, where they stand in the social order, how much they align and identify with their castes and caste identities, and how they are viewed or treated by others. Caste-based groups, divisions, and conflicts of interest exist at various levels and in various forms in educational institutions among students and faculties alike and in private and public institutions, government bodies, political and cultural organizations, business establishments, and so on. It can be discerned even in the Hindu communities who migrated from India long back and live abroad. Castes cannot be taken away from the thinking and actions of many Hindus, even if they are highly educated and know the virtues of equality and sameness. Even several swamis and spiritual gurus secretly indulge in it while speaking to the contrary. The upper castes, which today include many castes other than Brahmanas and Kshatriyas, enjoy relatively better social, political, and economic privileges, while in theory, the constitution guarantees equality and protection against discriminatory opportunities or treatment for everyone. Caste identities are still cherished by those who are benefited by them. Their influence can be seen in many aspects of India's social, political, economic, and cultural milieu, from films to politics. Compared to the past, the condition of the lower and oppressed castes has improved considerably due to the protections guaranteed by the law. However, the stench of the past still haunts many.

One may rewrite the history of ancient India and rationalize the caste system and the oppression and discrimination of lower castes that went on for a long time, glossing over facts and overwhelming voices of dissent. However, one cannot hide from the glaring truth that the caste system continues to be a disturbing aspect of Hinduism and a predominant source of discontent, dissonance, and disunion for all Hindus who practice it and identify themselves with it. Unless it is resolved with an enlightened approach and positive solutions, Hinduism will face headwinds in the coming times.

The idea of high (uccha) and low (nicha) births because of one's karma or divine justice has been an integral aspect of the Hindu social system and religious beliefs for millennia. Many Hindu scriptures justify and support the Varna system, claiming that the Creator Himself mandated it for the welfare, order, and regularity of the world. When they validate and approve of such an unjust system, and its continued practice, rational minds cannot help wondering how people can hold on to their beliefs and practice the faith without suffering from skepticism and indignation.

There are still many places in India where outcastes and lower castes are subject to discrimination and social injustice and where the ancient Varna system still exerts its waning influence, although it has outlived its purpose and is no longer aligned with the values of today. From school and college campuses to legislative bodies and government institutions, caste divisions, affiliations, and dynamics dominate India's collective psyche. Until they are swept away by the currents of modernity and the egalitarian values of equality and fraternity or universal brotherhood, Hinduism will remain vulnerable to the problem of conversions and desertion by those who feel discriminated against and experience feelings of isolation and alienation.

An Outline of the Four Main Varnas

The Vedic social order, consisting of four classes (varnas) of humans, is unique in the world but resembles, in some ways, Plato's ideal society of philosophers, warriors, and commoners. In the ancient world, Indian and Greek cultures had many common features. Probably for Greeks, Plato's social divisions, just as his doctrine of the world as a sum of ideas, remained mere philosophical concepts, but for Indians, they became a reality.

The word caste was originally used by the Portuguese and derived from the Portuguese word casta, which means race, breed, hereditary class, or group of people having the same ancestry. They used it to describe the social divisions that prevailed among the native people during their colonial rule in some parts of the Indian subcontinent. The present-day Hindu caste system was originally derived from this fourfold Vedic Varna system. Each Varna was a social division, class, or unit originally distinguished by the skin color (Varna), occupation, ancestry, and family lineage of its people. Probably, skin color became inconsequential, while other criteria remained as Vedism spread to various parts of India and assimilated many new groups and cultures. (The Varna system will be further explained in a subsequent chapter).

The Hindu law books (Dharma Shastras) codified the laws regarding the duties and conduct of each class and established a lasting foundation for the fourfold Varna system or social order that would help people perform their obligatory duties, ensure order and regularity of the world and achieve fulfillment, peace, harmony, and happiness for each class. They aimed to enforce this social order by drawing inferences from the Vedas and mandating it as the heavenly mandate. Creating a foundational basis, a set of obligatory rules, restraints, and a rigid code of conduct specific to each caste, the law books consolidated it further by making the varnas hereditary so that the social status of each newborn could be determined from birth. Subsequently, the fourfold Varna system gave way to a more complex caste system as numerous mixed castes emerged from the original four varnas, so much so that today, thousands of castes exist in India with no clarity about their origin, status, or connection to the original four. Due to the lack of historical records, they do not fit into the original fourfold Varna system. Their status depends upon local conditions and many social, cultural, and economic factors.

The original four classes

In the long history of Hinduism, the original fourfold Varna system of the Vedic period underwent many significant changes. The four distinct varnas do not exist today except in a diluted or vestigial form. Its place has been taken over by a complex caste system consisting of several groups (castes) and sub-groups (sub-castes). According to one estimate, presently, there are about 3,000 castes and 25,000 subcastes in India. The caste system's influence is so pervasive that social divisions and distinctions crept their way into other religions of India. Although some people trace their castes and family names to the Vedic Varna system, there are no definitive historical records to prove it.

It is also difficult to trace a person's genealogy based on last names or family names since they may be common to two or more castes. The more definitive social divisions that exist today are the ones between the upper and lower castes, the forward and backward castes, the scheduled and non-scheduled castes, and the scheduled tribes and scheduled castes. The government of India established some of these categories through the constitution and other legislations.

The Vedas and the Dharma Shastras declare that for the sake of the prosperity of the worlds, the Supreme Brahman created the Brahmanas, the Kshatriyas, the Vaisya, and the Sudra from His mouth, arms, thighs, and his feet, respectively, and assigned different functions to each of them. Dividing Himself into male and female parts, he manifested all creation. A brief description of each of these classes and their respective duties and responsibilities is provided below.

Brahmanas

By the original definition, Brahmanas are knowers of Brahman or those who perform sacrifices for Brahman, the highest, absolute, eternal, indestructible, supreme God. Since they were believed to emerge from the mouth of Brahman, they have the power to actualize their speech, wishes, or blessings by chanting and reciting the Vedas and invoking the gods through prayers and mantras during sacrifices. In the Vedic tradition, they represented the priestly class, who were entitled to study the Vedas, perform sacrificial rites and rituals for themselves and others, and, as householders, be obligated to perform certain obligatory duties, rituals, and sacraments. In the past, they performed priestly duties with fewer exceptions. Nowadays, they are engaged in various professions and occupations as priests, farmers, businesspeople, lawyers, doctors, merchants, chartered accountants, politicians, artists, artisans, soldiers, workers in farming, construction, engineering, transport, etc. The law books declare them as gods on earth. Those who serve as priests in temples and invoke gods on behalf of others through chants and rituals are like the intermediaries between gods and humans. The duty to uphold Dharma, preserve the faith, and exemplify the Hindu way of life rests with them.

According to Manu, the lawmaker, a Brahmana is an incarnation of Dharma (sacred tradition), born to serve and protect it as gods on earth. The typical Brahmana belongs to the excellent of the human race, who, by virtue of his karma and conduct, is rightfully endowed with purity, intelligence, and knowledge to attain Brahman. He is the highest among the beings on earth, a true representative of Brahma or Prajapati. Whatever existed in the world is his property and he is entitled to all. Thus, the tradition vests the pious Brahmanas with great authority, trust, and responsibility as the guardians and spokespersons of the faith. To them, God assigned the duties of "teaching and studying (the Veda), sacrificing for their own benefit and others, giving and accepting (of alms)." Of them, the best are those who know Brahman. They personify the eternal laws and are born to fulfill them. They also have the natural right to own and enjoy whatever they wish. At the same time, they have an onerous responsibility to live righteously, follow the sacred laws, and exemplify the highest virtues. Only they are qualified to be considered the true Brahmanas. In the past, apart from performing their priestly duties, they also served as teachers, counselors, ministers, and administrators in royal courts. Some became kings, and some served as warriors.

Kshatriyas

Kshatra means body, power, valor, wealth, military, rule, reigning order, etc. Kshatriyas represent all these qualities. They are the warrior class, who are commanded (by tradition) to serve as kings, rulers, administrators, ministers, soldiers, commanders, local heads, landlords, etc. Although in the caste hierarchy they ranked second, in the Vedic tradition, they were considered superior to Brahmanas in some respects. While the Brahmanas excelled in the knowledge of rituals (karma kanda), Kshatriyas excelled in the spiritual knowledge of the Self. Many Upanishadic seers and teachers were Kshatriyas. Kings like Janaka and Ajatashatru participated in spiritual knowledge. Their power declined subsequently, and many kings and emperors who ruled in the Indian subcontinent came from different castes. In its heydays, the Vedic religion was practiced and patronized by Kshatriya kings only. They worshipped Kshatriya gods such as Brahma, Indra, Soma, Varuna, Surya, Mitra, etc., whose power and prominence in the Vedic pantheon declined with the decline of the original, ancient Kshatriyas.

The lawbooks ordain them to protect people, bestow gifts to Brahmanas, offer sacrifices to gods and ancestors, study the Vedas, dispense justice, and ensure good governance, peace, and prosperity for all. According to Manusmriti, they abstain from sensual pleasures since, due to their rajasic nature, they are vulnerable to passions. Manu lays down that it is a king's obligatory duty to protect his kingdom and his people. He has something in himself of the nature of the gods such as Indra, Vayu, Yama, Surya, Varuna, Moon, and Kubera. Manu also advises people not to despise any king, even if he is an infant. His authority should not be questioned except when he ignores his duties or fails to uphold Dharma or protect pious Brahmanas. Kings and rulers have the right to punish, but they must be fair in delivering justice or prescribing punishments. A king must protect and uphold the caste system and the social order that comes with it as his obligatory duty and keep the Brahmanas happy with lavish and generous gifts at every opportunity.

Present-day Kshatriyas represent a diverse community of people belonging to different regions, cultures, castes, social strata, and linguistic regions. They are engaged in a wide range of occupations as merchants, politicians, businesspeople, industrialists, engineers, doctors, government employees, security personnel, technicians, soldiers, local chieftains, village heads, landlords, teachers, and professors. Many claim a historical connection with ancient lineages of Kshatriya families. However, historically, the ruling community of India did not belong to a particular caste or family lineage. The rules came from different backgrounds, some even from the lower caste.

Vaishyas

In the Vedic period, Vaishyas were predominantly land-owning and cattle-rearing farmers, merchants, and traders and performed duties associated with wealth generation through trade, commerce, agriculture, and other economic activities. In social hierarchy, Vaisyas stood next to Brahmanas and Kshatriyas. Like them, they were also considered twice-born (dvija) and allowed to study the Vedas and perform sacrifices. The law books ordain them to tend cattle, offer sacrifices to gods, study the Vedas, participate in trade and commerce, lend money, and cultivate the land. They have the traditional right to perform and participate in Vedic rituals and serve the community and gods through generous gifts and charitable works. However, they are not allowed to marry higher-caste women. According to Manu, a Vaisya must know the value of gems, pearls, coral, metals, clothes, perfumes, and condiments and must be acquainted with weights and measurements, assessing the quality of soils, sowing seeds, and raising crops. He must also know the languages of different regions and how to determine wages, assess the value of various commodities, and calculate the profit and loss of the merchandise with which he deals. In all such activities, he must strive to increase his wealth through rightful means, and with the wealth he earns, he must feed all living creatures.

Present-day Vaishyas belong to many castes and hail from different regions. Most of them are engaged in business, manufacturing, trade, and commercial activities. However, they also excel in several professions other than trade and commerce.

Shudras

In the social hierarchy, the Shudra class stood at the bottom of the Varna system. In the Vedic period, this group consisted of working people who served as artisans, craftsmen, agricultural workers, manual laborers, potters, domestic servants, gardeners, cattle herders, etc. They relied upon their physical strength and skills to serve others, which Manu declared was their main duty. The law books ordained them to serve the other three castes as their obligatory duty. They were not permitted to study or hear the sounds of the Vedas, chant the sacred hymns, or perform or participate in any Vedic rituals or samskaras. They were not allowed anywhere near the congregations where the Vedas were chanted, or religious subjects were discussed. They were also not allowed to mingle with the higher castes in social gatherings or eat food along with them. They might have worshipped local and village deities according to their family traditions.

Today, it is difficult to determine which of the castes belong to the original Shudra classifications. Some scholars incorrectly tend to lump all castes that are not Brahmanas, Kshatriyas, or Vaishyas under this category. However, it is not justified since many things have happened in the last two thousand years, and the original varnas lost their purity due to the intermixture of castes and integration of numerous non-Vedic groups into the original Vedic social order. Although the scriptures relegated the Shudras to a lower position in the caste hierarchy, they often enjoyed considerable power and prestige. History shows that although, in theory, the Vedic Varna system existed, in practice, people did not always choose professions according to their castes. According to some historians, Brahmanas often engaged in the duties of Kshatriyas. Those belonging to the lower rungs of society served in various positions as soldiers, archers, mahouts, personal attendants, merchants, herders, goatherds, traders, artisans, artists, administrators, and even rulers. It is difficult to determine whether they were considered Shudras by birth or due to their conversion from other religions, such

Chandalas

The lowest of the Shudras were called Chandalas. Some consider them to be the fifth Varna. It was a despicable and derogatory term, meaning the impure ones, since they engaged in impure professions such as cremators of corpses, hunters, butchers, trappers, and traders of animal skins and products. Some of them also engaged in armed robberies and dacoities. In the olden days, the higher castes looked down upon them as untouchables because of their unclean habits and unconventional religious practices that were outside the pale of the Vedic fold [1]. During the day, they were barred from entering the localities or neighborhoods where the higher castes lived or walking through the same streets they frequented. They were held in such contempt that people avoided even their shadow. If they saw them walking in public or crossing their paths, they considered it a bad omen. Due to such restrictions and superstitious beliefs, these deprived classes lived mostly on the fringes of society, unknown and uncared for. They, too, probably worshiped their gods and held to their own beliefs. They engaged in unclean professions avoided by the privileged classes, worked in graveyards and cremation grounds, or served as tanners, hunters, butchers, and professional cleaners of human waste[1]. While Shudras often rose to positions of power and prestige, owned lands, and served as kings and village heads, the position of Chandalas never improved. They were treated with disdain and barred from social gatherings and religious ceremonies.

How the Varna System Found Acceptance

The Hindu caste system is as old as the Vedic religion. It is a miracle that despite the absence of central leaders and an institution like an organized church, the caste system survived for at least three to four thousand years. It survived even when the Indian subcontinent was under Islamic and British rule, and people belonged to diverse social, religious, and cultural groups. Some scholars argue that the caste system was amplified and exploited by the British to further their interests, an argument that is not supported by many since there is ample evidence to believe that the system was a part of India's social fabric since ancient times. Indeed, it was not uniformly implemented everywhere as the land was ruled by many kings who were not all Hindus or did not practice any of its diverse traditions. It is also difficult to ascertain how far the law books exerted their influence upon people who were outside the pale of Vedic society and practiced their ancestral faiths that were not yet integrated into Vedism or other related traditions. In this chapter, we will examine how the caste system survived through the ages and what factors contributed to it.

In the past, the caste system was enforced by rulers and village panchayats, with the help of lawbooks such as Manusmriti and the authority vested in the kings, whom the tradition held as upholders and enforcers of Dharma and the divine laws ordained or endorsed by God himself. The provincial rulers, clan members, and local administrators wielded that power on their behalf and enforced the laws. The law books clearly laid down the privileges, duties, and obligations of each caste, stipulating punishments, and remedies for various offenses. The social and religious conditioning, force of habit, tradition, superstition, religious beliefs, social pressures, and fear of condemnation kept people in check and squashed any idea of opposing the norms and practices or upsetting the established status quo or class hierarchy. Of the many factors that reinforced the beliefs associated with the caste system - made it acceptable to a majority of Hindus and kept it alive in its long history, the following are worth

noting.
Religious beliefs

Beliefs associated with Dharma, Karma, rebirth, fate, divine retribution, fear of sin, etc., reinforced the belief that a person's caste and social and economic status were the fruit of one's karma. This belief made people accept their lot and take responsibility for it without questioning the scriptural injunctions, God, or the unjust caste system. The scriptures reinforced the belief that one could obtain a better birth and favorable circumstances in the next life only through auspicious actions. The Bhagavadgita explicitly states that evildoers God will cast evil-doers into evil wombs and subject them to suffering for their evil deeds. Such beliefs kept any opposition to the caste system under check. Those who were not happy with the system converted to Buddhism or Shaivism since these traditions opposed caste inequalities and disregarded many caste injunctions.

Heredity

The caste system was hereditary. A person's caste was determined at birth according to their parents' caste. This belief was reinforced by the fact that ancestors preferred to be reborn in the same families and lineages to which they belonged. Children derived their caste identity mainly from their fathers. If their mothers came from lower castes, children still enjoyed some caste privileges but were deemed inferior. Thus, people inherited their caste identities from their parents and passed them on to their children. They had no right to change their caste as long as they remained within the Vedic fold or served the community. Their kings, local administrators, or village heads had the authority to ostracize or excommunicate them from their original caste groups if they violated the caste norms or engaged in evil actions or scandalous conduct. In the case of inter-caste marriages, which were rare, children's inheritance rights and privileges were limited by the caste status of their mothers.

Caste Rules

The caste system was upheld in the past by a set of rules that varied for different castes and were strictly enforced by local religious and political authorities. Fear of punishment, social and family pressures, and public condemnation ensured the continuity of the system. Higher caste communities enjoyed many privileges, power, and authority but were also expected to live righteously and set good examples. For instance, Brahmanas were obligated to study the Vedas, perform sacrificial rituals, honor family traditions, and live righteously to secure a good life in their next lives. The lawbooks prescribed that Brahmanas who violated their code of conduct should be considered equal to Sudras and treated accordingly [2]. Upper-caste women were expected to assist their husbands in observing their caste rules and protecting the family's reputation. The law books also prescribed purification ceremonies, fines, and punishments, including excommunication in rare cases, to compensate for the loss of honor or nullify the sins arising from misconduct and caste violations.

Marriage

Since the caste system was based on heredity and the purity of their lineages, people paid close attention to the purity of their castes and family lineages to preserve their power, privileges, and authority and protect their honor and reputation in society. The law books upheld prevailing customs, traditions, caste, and cultural norms and discouraged people from marrying outside their castes, causing caste confusion. People, especially those from the upper castes, exercised enough social and family pressure upon themselves to prevent or discourage inter-caste marriages and inter-mixture of castes (varnasankara). Scriptures such as the Bhagavadgita allude to the fact that the Lord of Creation (Isvara) established a social order and the caste system to ensure the order and regularity of the world and prevent the intermixture of Varnas and the decline of Dharma. However, the law books contain provisions to accommodate certain types of inter-caste marriages and allow the children born out of them to regulate their lives, preserve family traditions and cultural norms, and enjoy inheritance rights. Inter-caste marriages between higher-caste men and women did not attract as much derision and social disapproval as those between higher-caste women and lower-caste men [3]. Adulterous relationships between them attracted serious punishments, including excommunication.

Caste privileges

Brahmans, Kshatriyas, and Vaishyas, the three upper castes, enjoyed distinct advantages in society compared to Shudras, whose job was to serve the three upper castes and live like fourth-class citizens [4]. The situation of Chandalas was even worse. People born in the three upper castes were given initiation into the study of the Vedas and treated as twice-born, while sudras were not allowed to study or even hear the Vedas. They were treated on par with animals and considered once born. Brahmanas enjoyed the highest status and privileges, followed by Kshatriyas, Vaishyas, and the Shudras in the same order. The laws prescribed discriminatory rewards and punishments for caste violations and criminal conduct. They recommended lighter punishments for higher castes than lower castes. Technically, the latter had little recourse against any accusations leveled against them other than leaving the matter entirely to the discretion of those who decided their cases. For the same offense committed, the lower caste accused could potentially attract physical torture, slavery, or the death penalty. In contrast, the higher caste ones could get away with rebuke, simple fines, and minor punishments or expiation rites for their transgressions. Deposition of lower caste people was not considered reliable and they were not allowed to give witness or sit in judgment against any cases involving higher castes.

Royal Support

The caste system was preserved and enforced mostly through royal support. The relationship between Brahmanas and Kshatriyas was one of symbiotic interdependence. Some scholars believe the Kshatriyas were at the top of the caste and social hierarchy before they were relegated to second place, which could be attributed to the decline of the original Kshatriya clans. Since then, the status of Brahmanas has remained unchallenged. As the guardians of Dharma, the kings and provincial rulers took upon themselves the duty of protecting and upholding the caste system and the privileges and obligations of each caste. By lending their support and protection and enforcing the laws, they ensured that caste distinctions, order, and regularity were maintained. From their side, Brahmanas supported their rulers, and administrators performed sacrifices for them, wishing them peace, prosperity, and victory in their wars. They also legitimized the rule of non-Kshatriya kings as the upholders and protectors of Dharma by performing ceremonies and redrawing their birth charts or tracing their ancestry to ancient lineages.

Manu proclaimed kings as gods in human form and protectors and preservers of castes (varnas) and the order of those who perform their obligatory duties [5]. He also stated that God created and gave the power of punishment to the kings on earth to help them destroy evil and keep humans on the Dharma's path [6]. He also prescribed that upon waking in the morning, a king should start his day by worshipping three Brahmanas and following their advice with humility and modesty. He should appoint a Brahmana as his chief minister and deliberate with him on the most important affairs of the State and his administration. A king who performs his duties and keeps his promise to the gods as the righteous upholder of Dharma and divine justice has the moral and temporal right and the authority to deliver judgments and inflict punishments.

Other factors

These were a few important factors that reinforced the caste system and ensured its widespread acceptance and continuity for several centuries. Other factors, such as fear of reappraisal, retaliation, or oppression from the higher castes, also prevented the lower castes from rebelling against the system and questioning its legitimacy. This has become the norm in today's world as many educated Indians are expressing their disapproval of it or the manner in which certain groups are treated by those in positions of power and authority. A few centuries ago, it could not even be contemplated, for the reprisal would have been severe. All the land, power, and economic resources rested with the higher castes and they literally owned those who worked for them. The dependence and penury also forced them to submit to the system and survive. Discrimination exists even today. In many regions of India, one can see the segregation of castes in villages where lower caste people live separately on the edges of the villages or adjacent to the farmlands. They are not prevented from entering the localities where higher castes live or entering their homes to perform some work or meet the owners. However, no one readily sells them any property or invites them as tenants.

A Brief History of the Varna System

The caste problem is a vast one, both theoretically and practically. Practically, it is an institution that portends tremendous consequences. It is a local problem, but one capable of much wider mischief, for "as long as caste in India does exist, Hindus will hardly intermarry or have any social intercourse with outsiders; and if Hindus migrate to other regions on earth, Indian caste would become a world problem. Dr. B.R. Ambedkar.

No one knows clearly the events that preceded or led to the origin and development of Indian civilization. All that we know for certain is that an ancient civilization called the Indus Valley Civilization thrived between 3000 BCE and 2000 BCE, although these dates are also speculative. It was followed by another civilization called the Vedic civilization. We do not know where these people came from. One of the views is that several nomadic and pastoral tribes, with extensive knowledge of elaborate sacrificial rites and rituals, migrated to the Indian subcontinent in the pre-Rigvedic or early Rigvedic period (about 2500 BCE) and established a unique civilization. They settled in the Northwestern region before they migrated further into the Gangetic Valley and the Deccan Plateau. Most likely, they gained power and prestige with their superior skills in warfare, cattle rearing, chariot-making, agriculture, organizational skills, and psychedelic magical rituals, coupled with their knowledge of horses, hunting, chariot-making, astronomy, metallurgy, healing, medicinal plants, farming, etc.

They also belonged to several warrior tribes who initially fought among themselves. The Bharatas, who emerged victorious in the internecine wars, were the most prominent among them. Their kings seem to have gained an upper hand in the power struggle and ruled large tracts of land in the northwest. They patronized the Vedic religion, participated in philosophical debates and discussions, and contributed to the development of the Upanishadic philosophy. By adapting and embracing local beliefs, gods, customs, and practices and integrating them into their own and by recruiting the local warrior groups into their militaries, they likely gained the confidence of the local populations in the Gangetic plain who had already settled there and practiced different faiths. With these developments, the fourfold Varna system probably became imperative and rigid as Vedic religion spread further into the subcontinent, attracting new groups and populations into its fold.

The non-Vedic character of the Varna system

The pastoral Vedic tribes who migrated from outside India probably did not introduce the rigid caste system. They likely had a flexible social structure in which people from different social backgrounds coexisted and had the freedom to change their vocations according to circumstances. The Vedas allude to the fact that members within the same families often practiced different vocations. Even Brahmanas had the option to choose a different vocation in exceptional circumstances like wars, famines, and pestilence. It could be that a rudimentary form of caste system was already in vogue in ancient India [7]. Most likely, the Vedic people of that transformative period adopted it to maintain their racial purity, family lineages, and societal order. This is evident from the fact that there is no reference to the caste system in the entire Rigveda except in the Purusha Sukta, which many scholars believe was a later day interpolation.

The Mahabharata and Ramayana are classic examples of how people from different social, tribal, and cultural backgrounds coexisted in the Indian subcontinent and played different roles in society in spite of caste barriers and religious instructions. The Varna system had taken root. However, people seemed to have some freedom to choose their professions. For example, Parashurama and Drona were Brahmanas. Yet, they became warriors and excelled in the art of warfare. Vishwamitra [8], a warrior by birth, became a great seer. Shantanu, a King, married a fisherwoman. The same fisherwoman had an amorous encounter with a seer who was smitten by her beauty. Bhima married a tribal woman and had a son named Ghatothkach through her. Karna was the adopted son of a charioteer. Yet, Duryodhana accepted him as a close friend and gifted him a kingdom to elevate his status. Kings like Janaka participated in religious and spiritual discussions and gave generous gifts to Brahmanas. Many Upanishadic teachers were warriors. They admitted Brahmana students and taught them secret knowledge. Valmiki, the composer of the Ramayana, was a hunter by profession. Subsequently, the caste system probably became rigid in an effort to protect the tradition and preserve its purity and integrity due to changing economic, environmental, and demographic circumstances and interactions and conflicts with hostile tribes and competing religious traditions. Yet, the tradition could not remain immune to outside influences, as is evident from the fact that it accepted the Atharva Veda, which is predominantly non-Vedic in character, as the fourth Vedas, besides admitting many new gods and goddesses into its pantheon along with their associated beliefs, doctrines, and ritual practices.

Varna in Hindu Epics and Puranas

We have already quoted instances from the Hindu epics and Puranas to suggest that the Varna system could have been flexible in the initial stages and allowed people to follow their natural inclinations and choose vocations not prescribed for their castes. We also find in them instances where people could rise to positions of eminence and authority through sheer effort or personal skills. Their examples confirm that people could transcend caste-based rules and scriptural injunctions and change their circumstances or improve their social standing by proving themselves. Many important characters in the epics Ramayana and Mahabharata belonged to lower castes. The epics and the Puranas contain numerous instances. The epic Ramayana illustrates how people of humble origins and outlier communities helped Lord Rama cross the ocean, defeat the mighty Ravana, and rejoin his wife, Sita. Lord Rama's mother, Kausalya, probably belonged to the family of a tribal ruler from the adjoining regions of Dandakaranya, where Lord Rama spent much of his exile. A temple in her name still exists in the Raipur District of Chhattisgarh. Due to the strange circumstances surrounding his birth, Lord Krishna grew up in a family of cowherds, as his birth parents wanted to protect him from his notoriously evil uncle Kamasa. Balarama, his stepbrother, who is sometimes included in the list of Vishnu's ten incarnations, was both a farmer and a warrior. Of the ten incarnations of Lord Vishnu, only three or four incarnations belonged to the higher castes. Of the ten, only two, the incarnations of Vamana and Parasurama, were Brahmanas. Parasurama was a Brahman by birth and Kshatriya by profession. Lord Rama and Buddha were Kshatriyas by birth, while the other incarnations, such as the incarnation of fish, turtle, boar, and the half man and half lion, are animal or nonhuman incarnations. In other words, most incarnations were not high-born or twice-born (dvija) according to the Vedic caste rules.

Many ancient sages and rishis also came from diverse and humble backgrounds. Their lives and achievements show the inclusivity and social adjustment accommodated by the tradition in the age of the epics and the Puranas. Parasurama was a Brahmana by birth but adopted the Kshatriya Dharma. Vishwamitra [2] was a Kshatriya by birth but lived like a true Brahmana and seer, practicing austerities and karma sannyasa. Sage Parashar, a famous lawgiver, was the son of an outcaste (Chandala). Rishi Vashista was born to a prostitute, while sage Vyasa, the original author of the Mahabharata, was born to a fisherwoman. Rishi Valmiki, the original composer of Ramayana, came from a tribal family of traditional hunters. Some composers of the Vedic and Upanishadic hymns belonged to either lower castes or mixed castes. Satyakama Jabala was born to a servant maid who did not know who his father was since, as a maid, she was obligated to fulfill the wishes of the men in whose households she worked. A family of charioteers took care of Karna, the son of Kunti and the abandoned brother of Pandavas, as his foster parents, while Drona was a Brahmana by caste but a Kshatriya by profession. He trained both Pandavas and Kauravas in martial arts and military tactics.

The development of a rigid social system

Although we cannot be certain, the caste system or the Varna system of the early Vedic period was probably hereditary but not as rigid as it became subsequently in the post-Gupta period (sixth century CE). People still had an opportunity to practice different vocations or deviate from their family or hereditary occupations and fulfill their obligations in the pursuit of the four chief aims: Dharma, Artha, Kama, and Moksha. Perhaps the duties of Brahmanas were exclusively reserved for them, whereas no such limitations seemed to have applied to the other three castes. The status of each caste was also solidified in the social order, at least by the time the Ramayana and Mahabharata were composed.

As the caste boundaries and code of conduct for each caster were clearly established, marriages within the same varnas must have become the norm, in which compatibility of the bride and groom was determined by their respective birth charts, varnas (caste or kulam), jatis (a group distinguished by linguistic, tribal, cultural, regional, or religious practice), family lineages, and gotras. The varnas were initially said to be three. Subsequently, they became four with the inclusion of people from different cultures and backgrounds, which added to the complexity and heterogeneity of the Vedic society. With the growing complexity and diversity of populations, attempts were probably made to protect and preserve the purity and integrity of each caste and ensure order and regularity by codifying the laws and making the caste (Varna), family (kula), and community (jati) central to social and economic relationships, activities and development. Thus, parentage, family history, and lineage might have gained more importance in public and personal relationships than occupation.

Because of such factors, the caste or Varna system, which came into existence in the early Vedic period, might have subsequently become rigid and less accommodative after the Guptas, offering little flexibility to people to pursue different vocations outside their hereditary roles or family occupations as determined by their castes. The lack of teachers willing to teach children of other families or unrelated families the secrets of their family vocations for economic or social reasons could be an additional factor. Foreign invasions, immigration, demographic changes, the addition of many foreign groups, each with distinct cultural and religious practices, and increasing social and communal tensions and conflicts of interest might have prompted caste to safeguard their personal, occupational, and social privileges and prevent the possibility of the intermixture of castes, caste pollution, and confusion. The law books (Dharma Shastras) filled that need. They established a well-defined code of conduct, a set of rewards and punishments, purification procedures, and religious practices -invoking the authority of the

Vedas - to protect the privileges of each caste or Varna and ensure social harmony, order, and peaceful coexistence of diverse communities.

Elevation of the Sudra Kings

Contrary to popular belief, many emperors and rulers in ancient India did not descend from the original Kshatriya clans of the early Vedic period or the Rigvedic period. Many belonged to diverse and often humble backgrounds. Some of them were probably not even connected to the original pastoral or warring tribes who migrated from outside but likely descended from those who were already well-settled in the subcontinent by the time the Vedic civilization took shape, and people were gradually migrating further from the Sindhu-Saraswathi region into the hinterland. This new breed of warriors, driven by personal courage and an adventurous spirit, established many small kingdoms in the northwest and adjoining areas and often fought among themselves. They eventually gave birth to several small principalities called Janapadas, each with its distinct geographical boundaries, history, ruling dynasties, and political systems. The Vedas, epics, Puranas, and Buddhist and Jain texts mention the names of several Janapadas. Some had hereditary kings, and some elected their kings through a council of influential people. Most of them were not Kshatriyas but belonged to different social backgrounds. Most likely, they also practiced different faiths, including Buddhism and Jainism.

Subsequently, these small kingdoms yielded larger and more powerful kingdoms, such as those of the Kurus, Yadus, and Panchalas. According to the Mahabharata, although the Kauravas and Pandavas belonged to the Kshatriya lineage of the Bharatas, they were of mixed origin due to their birth under strange circumstances. The Shishunaga and Haranyaka dynasties, who ruled large kingdoms in northern India between the sixth and fifth century BCE, also came from mixed backgrounds. The Nandas, who established a vast Magadhan empire with Pataliputra as their capital in the fourth or fifth century BCE, belonged to a family of barbers. The Mauryas who succeeded them also belonged to humble backgrounds. Chandragupta Maurya, who many classical historians regard as the first true emperor of India, was said to have descended from a family of peacock tamers. According to legends, his mother served in the court of Nandas as a courtesan and sired him through one of the Nandas. Chandragupta Maurya himself married princesses from different social and cultural backgrounds, including one from Greece. We do not know whether he practiced the Vedic religion, but at the time of his death, he was certainly converted to Jainism and died as a Jain monk.

The Sakas and the Kushanas were foreigners with no Kshatriya, Vedic, or Indian heritage. They descended from the nomadic tribes of Central Asia and practiced varied faiths. Some patronized Shaivism but kept away from Vedism. The Guptas, who also established a Magadha empire, were believed to be either Vaishyas or Jats [9], while the Nagas or the Barashivas ruled from central India were tribals and, by Vedic designation, Sudras. The intriguing aspect is how the Vedic priests of their times managed their relationship with these kings and foreign rulers who were not conversant with their ritual and spiritual beliefs and practices and held different belief systems. In most cases, these rulers stayed away from Vedism. They preferred Buddhism, Jainism, or Shaivism, which did not discriminate against people on the basis of their birth, profession, color, or caste. Some of them might have accepted the recognition offered by the Vedic priests in return for gifts and land grants to convert and legitimize them as Kshatriyas, using purification and conversion rituals and tracing their lineages to gods, ancient rulers, and races of divine or semi-divine origins. If these strategies failed, the priestly families kept a low profile or migrated to safer areas to avoid public attention.

Varna, Jāti and Gotra

Before we go into details, let us define these three words: Varna, Jāti, and Gotra. Varna means color. The Varna system of the Vedic times was a precursor of the social system that subsequently emerged in India as the present-day caste system [10] and grew in complexity. The Varna system recognized the division of the population into four distinct groups based on occupations and, perhaps, at least in the initial stages, differences in skin color. Jāti refers to a community of people distinguished by a common language, culture, origin, interpersonal relationships, beliefs, and geographic, tribal, or racial identity. The word is rather vague and can be used differently in different circumstances. For example, all the people of India can be considered one jāti, the Bharata jāti. At the same time, one may distinguish between different jatis within it, such as Telugu jāti, Tamil jāti, and so on. Gotra refers to a person's family lineage and historical connection with the lineages of Brahmanas, who used to perform rituals for the family. It may also refer to the names of the cow pens (gotra) people used in the Vedic period or later to keep their cattle or the specific names they used to brand their cows. Today, it is mostly used to distinguish the lineages of the devotees before the deities during ritual worship and sacrificial ceremonies. The gotras of a bride and bridegroom are invariably ascertained to ensure that they belong to different ancestral lines since the tradition explicitly prohibits marriages between the same gotras or connected lineages.

Early Vedic society likely had social divisions based primarily on color and family lineages and secondarily on occupations. This is evident from the Rigvedic hymns, which distinguish people based on their complexion and creed rather than occupation-based castes. A well-defined social order based on the four classes must have existed, but we do not know how rigidly it was enforced since we do not know the control systems that were in force or had the authority to enforce it. The cast system[10] is known in Sanskrit as varnashrama dharma, which actually means a natural social order based on color distinctions. Initially, the four classes might have come into existence due to the differences in the color of the skin. As time went by, the name remained, but skin color might have become a nonissue. In the early days, a Brahmana was considered a varnashresht the best of all. Varna also meant a letter, character, or sound. Teaching how to write and spell Sanskrit letters was called Varna-shiksha. People were distinguished by their skin color and contrasted with the dark-skinned ones, known as Daityas, Dasas, Asuras, Pisachas, and Rakshasas. They were probably derisive terms used to refer to certain outlier groups with whom they had no cordial relations or whose beliefs and practices they did not appreciate. Some scholars believe that varnas are not the same as castes. Varnas were classes based on racial features, while castes were divisions within each class based on occupations or lineages. Thus, while there were only four varnas or classes, the number of castes or occupational divisions within each class varied.

The word jati actually means the form of existence that comes by birth. Thus, animals belong to pasujati, or the animal group, and humans to narajati, or the human group. Jati is also used loosely to mean a caste, a regional or linguistic group, race, lineage, tribe, or class of humans. A jati-Brahmana is someone who is a Brahmana by birth but not by occupation, knowledge, or performance of rites and rituals. The words jat, meaning birth or existence, and jatakam, meaning natal chart, are closely related to it.

Gotra actually means the name of a cow pen or a stable. It is also used to denote the name of a family, lineage, or race of Brahmana families. Strictly speaking, only Brahmana families are supposed to belong to particular gotras. In the case of people belonging to other castes, it denotes the lineage of their respective family priests. Therefore, when a non-Brahmana is quoting his gotra, he is telling the gotra of the priest whose services his family traditionally used. Traditionally, the gotras of Brahmana families are traceable to seven or eight ancient sages. However, today, there are thousands of gotras, and no one knows how these many gotras have sprouted. For Brahmana families, gotras are significant. However, in other caste groups, gotras matter, especially in ritual worship and the performance of sacraments. Marriages within the same gotra are prohibited by the law books just as they are prohibited in the case of castes.

Subsequent Developments

The Indian society was as complex in ancient India as it is now. Any generalizations about it need to be regarded with some reservations. The political, geographic, and linguistic diversity, absence of adequate dependable historical evidence, contradictory literary sources, and the existence of multiple religious traditions make it a daunting task for any writer to present a satisfactory picture of the prevailing conditions of Indian society at any point of time in the past. In the following discussion, we will try to sketch a broad outline of how the caste system might have developed in the post-Vedic period.

During the Mauryan period (300 BC), while the varnas remained four, the castes became many. Inter-caste marriages, the practice of polygamy, the assimilation of foreigners, the creation of vast administrative machinery that resulted in new classes of people and new positions of authority, and the geographical expansion of the empires to the south, which exposed new groups and communities to the Vedic religion contributed to this new development and added diversity and complexity to the social fabric of ancient India. Megasthanese, who stayed in the court of Chandragupta Maurya as a Greek ambassador for several years, recorded his observations in his work titled During his stay. He noticed seven classes of people in the Mauryan empire.

1. Philosophers
2. Husbandmen
3. Shepherds
4. Artisans
5. Military
6. Overseers
7. Councilors or Assessors

There were further sub-divisions within each of these classes. Megasthanese identified two distinct divisions within the philosopher's group: the priests and the ascetics. In the Satavahana empire, society was organized into four classes [111].

1. **First class**: high-ranking officials and feudatory chieftains such as Maharathis, Mahabhojas, and Mahasenapatis.
2. **Second class**: officials such as ministers and treasurers (Amatyas, Mahamatras, and Bhandagarikas) and non-officials such as merchants, traders, and heads of guilds (Naigama, Sarthvaha and Sreshtin).
3. **Third class**: professionals such as scribes (lekhakas), physicians (vaidyas), cultivators (halakiyas), goldsmiths (suvarnakaras), and chemists (gandhikas).

4. **Fourth class**: carpenters (vardhaki), gardeners (malakaras), blacksmiths (lohavanija), and fishermen (dasakas).

The Guptas worshipped Hindu deities, built temples in their honor, and revived many ancient Vedic traditions. They enforced the caste system throughout their empire with religious zeal. They implemented many traditions of Vedic religion as a part of the king's duty to uphold and protect religious laws (dharma) and safeguard the caste system from the unlawful intermixture of castes. The Brahmanas, who enjoyed many privileges under their patronage, were known for their austere lives. There were many groups within the priestly class, each performing specific duties. They studied the scriptures, performed sacrifices and devotional worship, and observed penances to control their minds and bodies. The kings lavished them with gifts and land grants, often donating entire villages in return for their services. People revered saints and the places associated with their lives. The kings employed royal priests in their courts and consulted them frequently. Brahmanas of this period belonged to many lineages or gotras.

The Guptas brought peace and prosperity to the Indian subcontinent and contributed to the emergence of new aristocratic classes. Their period witnessed the development of new elite groups, as in the Roman empire, an urban version of the bourgeoisie consisting of wealthy traders, merchants, and landed gentry owning large tracts of fertile lands fit for agriculture. These groups engaged in a new power struggle among themselves for royal favors, which added additional dynamics and diversity to the already complex caste system and social structure. Brahmanas kept their dominance and authority in religious matters, while the feudal groups exercised their control over wealth creation, trade and commerce. The status of the lower castes depended upon their occupation and religious affiliation. Artisans, skilled workers of arts and crafts, and other vocational groups had their guilds to manage and regulate their activities and protect their interests.

Conquests and the resulting wars with the invading armies, such as the Hunas, in the declining phase of the Gupta rule, led to many new developments within Indian society. As soldiers of invading armies settled in India's heartland, the caste system faced new challenges. According to Havell, the infusion of Huna blood lowered the high ethical standards of Indo-Aryan traditions. It caused the growth of many vulgar superstitions, which the great teachers of India never contradicted. The intolerance of the Hunas only added to the rigidity of the caste system in the subsequent period as a defensive reaction, just as the intolerant attitude of Muslim rulers contributed to a rigid caste system during the medieval period.

Hsüen Tsang (Xuanzang), who visited India during the reign of Harshavardhana, noticed that the caste system was widely prevalent and practiced in the country. He noticed four distinct social classes, most likely a continuation of the Vedic fourfold Varna system. The Brahmanas and the Kshatriyas of that time lived a good life, dressed well, ate decent meals, and observed high standards of cleanliness. He noted that after eating food, they destroyed the wooden and stone vessels they used to eat it. If they used metal ones, they cleaned them thoroughly. They maintained high ethical standards and dreaded the retribution of bad karma. Inter-caste marriages and marriages within the same caste or among close relations were absent. However, caste distinctions, food restrictions, and marriage customs did not prevent people of different castes from interacting socially or living in harmony. He also noticed the sad plight of the outcasts and commented that they were not allowed to enter the localities where the higher caste people lived or walked through.

We may presume these practices continued for the next several centuries and even during the Muslim rule. The caste system continued during the medieval period despite the oppressive policies of Muslim rule. Despite its universal appeal and emphasis on brotherhood, neither Islam nor the bigotry of the invaders left much impact on the caste system, the native faiths, or the beliefs and practices of the native people. The caste system and the beliefs that sustained it actually helped them survive this turbulent period. They strengthened their resolve to adhere to their ancestral faiths despite the attempts to convert them forcibly. Some rulers discriminated against them, imposed additional taxes on their households as per Islamic laws, and humiliated higher-caste Hindus by forcing them to work in Muslim households as servants after reducing them to utter poverty through unjust taxation. They also succeeded in converting a few, especially those from the less privileged castes, by offering them incentives or using threats. Some rulers made it their policy to put to death a certain number of natives each year to strike fear in their hearts and weaken their resolve to follow their native faiths. These actions had the opposite effect. They made the caste system even more rigid and people more loyal to their family traditions and ancient faiths. Those who switched their loyalties (usually from the lower castes) became as distant and repugnant as the invaders in the eyes of those who endured the ignominy and the oppression silently. Interestingly, the caste system left its ancient mark even on the communities that emerged in the wake of conversions under Islamic rule. A new social structure and class divisions emerged among them according to their descent, vocations, or old caste affiliations, adding a new social dimension to the Muslim community in the country. Some scholars believe the Muslim rulers adopted the caste system as a "compromise" to keep their subjects under control.

When the Europeans came to India first as merchants and later as conquerors, they followed a similar policy. The British, who subsequently established their direct rule in several Indian provinces, used the Indian caste system to consolidate their power and formulate their civil and criminal laws. They also used it to implement their dive and rule policy and consolidate their power and influence over the native populations. They decided to let the caste system prevail as they saw it as a great opportunity to keep the people divided on caste and religious lines and maintain their hold upon them. They also organized their military units on caste lines to ensure discipline, unity, and caste loyalties among the recruits. The Christian missionaries who came to India in their wake to convert local people found the caste system convenient for spreading negative propaganda against the native faiths and converting people to their faith. They succeeded to some extent as their activities remained unchecked for a long time as the British authorities made no efforts to contain them due to their policy of non-interference in the country's religious matters. However, as time went by, the educated Indian middle class, one of the unintended consequences of the British education system, responded to the growing threat from them and responded with countermeasures. Many nationalist leaders of the freedom struggle felt the need to reform and revive Hinduism and address the threat posed by its antique practices, especially the caste system and the excessive focus on superstitious beliefs and ritual practices. They urged the community to treat everyone fairly and discontinue the outdated social practices of inequality and discrimination against the deprived castes in the interests of preserving and safeguarding Hinduism and the community. Indian scholars revived memories of India's past glory and its rich social, cultural, and literary greatness to instill feelings of pride and nationalism in people. Leaders like Baba Saheb Ambedkar and Raja Rammohan Roy demanded equal status for the lower castes, while Mahatma Gandhi advocated equal rights for all and the complete abolition of untouchability.

After India's independence, the Indian Constitution guaranteed equal status and fundamental rights to all classes of people. They also enacted legislation to prevent the continuation of many ancient practices, such as polygamy and discrimination based on caste or religion. The government passed laws to declare untouchability as a serious crime, punishable with severe penalties and created a list of scheduled castes and tribes to protect them from exploitation and ill-treatment. The reservation policy approved by the Parliament created a level playing field for them in matters of employment and education. It protected them from unfair competition from the more privileged sections of society. Due to these efforts and the enforcement of policies, the lower castes are improving their standing in various fields. Today, many belonging to these castes occupy positions of authority and leadership in politics, government jobs, business, trade, and commerce, contributing to the development of the country. The Indian government established many built-in safeguards and constitutional guarantees for them and considerably improved their status in society. As a result, the high castes often complain of being discriminated against and subjected to unequal treatment in jobs, economic benefits, and welfare measures. By granting constitutional guarantees to the lower castes and protecting them from unfair competition, the Indian government averted a major disaster for independent India. These efforts minimized the possibility of social unrest, prevented a civil war, and halted mass conversions of the discriminated groups to other religions. However, further improvement and reforms are still required to improve their lot and change people's thinking and attitude towards them. People still value their caste identities and make judgments and decisions based on them. Caste is still a powerful binding force in politics, economics, social activities, and personal relationships.

A Critical Analysis

The Hindu caste System has long been one of Hinduism's main weaknesses. In the past, it seemed to have helped communities weather storms and upheavals and preserve their faith and family traditions. However, in today's world and the value system we uphold, it has become a source of strife, conflict, disunity, and cause for concern. It has also been exploited by some for selfish ends or to proselytize Hindus to other faiths. In terms of impact, it caused greater damage for a much longer period to a great many people than the slave system of the Western world or the crusades, persecutions, and inquisitions of medieval Europe. The Hindu caste system was a clever invention of the later Vedic society, justified by a few lawmakers who wanted to create a viable social structure rooted in dogma and conditioned beliefs to preserve their faith, wealth, status, privileges, practices, monopolies, and way of life. People who belonged to the upper castes found it convenient to retain and perpetuate their social and religious distinction and political and economic control and advantage. Except for Shaivism and a few ascetic traditions, most sectarian traditions of Hinduism accepted the caste system as a divine injunction or a consequential aspect of one's fate (vidhi), actions (karma), and Nature's diversity (Prakriti Dharma).

The idea of staying away from unclean and unkempt people is understandable in a world that was obsessed with the fear of death and the concept of physical and mental purity. There is nothing unusual about people being wise and selective in choosing their friends and relationships or staying away from strangers and staying within their comfort zones. It is normal human behavior to stay away from people who are perceived or feared to be socially deviant, untrustworthy, unfamiliar, or dangerous. It is an expression of our social intelligence and self-preservation instinct. Personal hygiene, family background, and financial status do matter today in our personal and social relationships as it was thousands of years ago. But what was wrong with the Vedic caste system was that it recognized inequalities based on birth, hereditary, and family lineages of men and proclaimed it to be the will of God. Vedic scholars perpetuated this line of thought and hereditary caste system for centuries, quoting the authority of scriptures and invoking fear of divine retribution. They created human stereotypes to justify a social structure that favored a few at the expense of many, preserving their social, economic, and political privileges and denying a vast majority of people opportunities and freedom to use their inborn strengths, talents, and abilities, and pursue their dreams and aspirations. It gave little hope to those who were stuck at the bottom of the social hierarchy and conditioned by centuries of prejudice to accept and obey that unequal system.

Hinduism is a universal religion. Its primary emphasis is on universal brotherhood. It declares the world as one divine family and all humans and all the creatures (jivas), big and small, as a part of it. The material universe is compared to God's body and His consciousness and supreme intelligence to our transcendental, pure consciousness, and intelligence. It believes that all humans are divine by nature and connected to the gods, the Creator Himself, and the rest of creation through their divine nature. Realizing the supreme truth that each is a minor replica of the Supreme Lord of Creation and dissolving oneself into that cosmic identity and sacred thought is supposed to be the primary aim of all human activity.

However, with such lofty ideals, it is rather unfortunate that for an exceedingly long time, this religion of great antiquity has been under the hegemony of a few privileged castes who prevailed upon natural human instincts and weaknesses to foist and perpetuate a system that was explicitly favorable to them. Drawing strength from numerous authoritative sources, many beliefs and practices associated with it have taken deep roots in Hindu culture and psyche and persist even today in various forms. Caste identity is an integral part of a Hindu's personal and family identity. It determines many aspects of their living conditions, education, profession, marriage, friendships, support system, social standing, career, influence, image, chances of success, alliances, opportunities, and so on. Caste prejudice, explicit or implied, is still a persistent problem in many countries where Hindus are a majority. Perhaps there are no other nations in the world where social divisions find traditional, cultural, and scriptural acceptance, approval, and validation on a large scale. People who are born in upper caste families enjoy relatively better lives and social and economic privileges than those born in the lower castes. It is not that all upper-caste Hindus are entitled to them or that economic disparities do not exist among them. However, compared to their counterparts, they enjoy better status and privileges than others, even with economic or social disadvantages. Within the same social milieus, upper-caste families enjoy relatively better opportunities and opportunities to grow. At the same time, we cannot ignore that when we generalize large groups and populations, there will be exceptions and anomalies.

In the Vedic age, at least in the initial phases, the caste system was not very rigid since "there was no privileged order of priests." During this time, the word Vaishya denoted all the people in the region irrespective of their profession and lineage. There was a rudimentary form of caste system in which a person's caste depended not upon his birth but upon his profession, as is evident from some of the hymns of the Rigveda (9.112.3). According to one textbook on Ancient India by V.C. Pandey and U.S. Khattri, I read long back, even during the Gupta Period (200-600 CE), the Hindu society consisted of Vaishyas and Sudras. Although contemporary literature of that period seems to present a more rigid caste system, in practical terms, it was flexible. According to another historian, Sri Nahar, the rigidity of the caste system probably began during this period. People did not take up occupations according to their varnas. Except for the Sudras, people of other varnas mingled freely and dined and drank together. Sudras were not confined to serving others only but took the professions of agriculture and trade. Indeed, this is the condition even today. Except for the priestly duties which are still performed mostly by Brahmana priests only, all other professions are open to everybody in the Hindu society.

Historians tend to quote many reasons for the emergence of the hereditary caste system as a defining aspect of Vedic society in ancient India. Chaotic conditions, wars, insecurity, and frequent migrations could have been one reason. The most plausible and accepted theory is that the Vedic people probably found the heredity or family status of a person and a social order based on it as a convenient solution to preserve their traditions and family lineages while adapting to live in close proximity to other cultures and a heterogeneous population who practiced different faiths. India had diversified demographics then as it is now. The hereditary caste system might have proven useful in preserving the social order and the Vedic Dharma as these diverse groups adapted to their faith and way of life. There is no doubt that, subsequently, the caste system became rigid based on a person's birth rather than any other factor, although we cannot be sure that it was the case everywhere. Its rigidity and how strictly it was enforced probably depended upon several factors. It might have been enforced strictly if the rulers honored the Dharma Shastras and took upon themselves the duties of protecting and upholding the Vedic Dharma. Where the rulers had other aims and practiced other faiths, probably the higher castes kept their practices to themselves and avoided contact with other people. Where it prevailed, it allowed the priestly classes to keep their dominance and influence and enjoy social and economic privileges.

Brahmana truly means knower of Brahman or one who knows how to communicate with Brahman and invoke His powers through sacrifices and Vedic chants. By definition, the children of a Brahmana do not become Brahmanas. They become so only if they possess the knowledge of Brahman and the ways to realize Him within themselves. Mere birth does not lead to self-realization but only persistent, spiritual effort. The Vedas personify Brahman. Those who know the Vedas and the specific mantras used to invoke gods are truly qualified to be Brahmanas. They are like gods on earth since they know how to communicate with gods, obtain their blessings, and help their patrons fulfill their desires and wishes. In the past, such powers or claims gave Brahmanas an exceptional opportunity to win the favor of their rulers and patrons, establish a strong rapport with them, and earn rich gifts and grants from them.

Their relationship with Kshatriyas and Vaishyas was one of equality. Kshatriyas possessed political power, and Vaishyas possessed economic power. Brahmanas, with their knowledge, power, and spiritual authority, helped them both by helping them consolidate their political and economic powers by performing sacrifices for them and helping them achieve their aims of Dharma, Artha, Kama, and Moksha. The Shudras were needed since, without them, none of the aims could be fulfilled. Kings needed them for their armies, taxes, security, law and order, and other administrative tasks. Traders and merchants needed them for their commercial and business activities. Therefore, their admission into the Vedic fold became a social, political, and economic necessity to ensure progress, order, and regularity. It is doubtful they could secure their help and cooperation without treating them fairly. Therefore, they most likely maintained cordial relationships with the gentry and lived in harmony with them. At the time, through the invention of various laws, they restricted their social and economic advancement and their equation with other groups.

For their part, the Brahmanas enjoyed their privileges, keeping a rigid control over the knowledge of the Vedas and sacrificial duties and how that knowledge was shared with the other groups. The scriptures also helped them by legitimizing their claims, limiting their reach to the higher castes, and designating them as the guardians of the Dharma. For example, the Purusha Sukta of the Rigveda (10.90), a hymn that describes the origin of the four varnas, clearly establishes and validates the superiority of the upper three varnas as a divine injunction, suggesting that Brahmanas emerged Brahman's head, personifying His speech and intelligence, Kshatriyas from His shoulders personifying His physical prowess, and Vaishyas from His belly, personifying wealth. It declares that the Shudras as the lowest of all, suggesting that they emerged from His feet. The fact is that just as a person will be crippled and cannot move, society cannot move or progress without the Shudras contributing their labor.

Despite hymns that justify humanity's division into four distinct classes, the Vedas do not explicitly approve the hereditary caste system or confer any privileges or special powers on any particular group or caste. In fact, they repeatedly affirm the equality of all, stating that Brahman is the Self of all, exists in all, and all are equal and part of His universal divine family. They do not mandate a rigid caste system or discrimination of people according to their birth, color, caste, or occupation. The Dharma Shastras, however, quoted the Vedas and invoked their authority to justify the hereditary caste system and prescribe a specific code of conduct for each caste, thereby legitimizing the inequality and discrimination that arose from it and giving it the semblance of divine law.

Since the Vedas were considered inviolable and the final authority in all matters, other scriptures followed their example and justified the system. Hence, in the secondary scriptures, such as the Bhagavadgita or the Puranas, we find references to the hereditary caste system peculiarly out of context, even if such assertions contradicted the essential concepts such as oneness, sameness, renunciation, and liberation they preached. The Bhagavadgita explicitly implies that a person's caste is determined at birth while claiming at the same time that God treats everyone equally and all are welcome to worship Him and attain liberation. For example, in one verse (1.42), Lord Krishna states that when women become impure and fall into evil ways, with the intermixture of castes arising from it, they and their families will descend into hell. Because of their misdeed, Dharma will perish. In the third chapter (3.24), he says that if he does not perform his duties, he will become the cause of the confusion of castes and undue harm to humanity. In the fourth chapter (4.13), he says that he created the four castes based on the division of duties. (He does not say that he created them based on their birth). In the sixteenth chapter, he says that he casts evil doers in demonic wombs. Obtaining those demonic wombs, birth after birth, they fail to reach him.

All these assertions legitimize the hereditary caste system and give it the semblance of divine approval. We do not know whether they were genuinely original or latter-day interpolations to reinforce and justify the system or the social practice. We cannot help wondering about their veracity when we view them in the context of the fact that Lord Krishna himself grew up in a pastoral community of cowherds (Shudras) and was neither a Kshatriya nor Brahmana by birth. He was a Kshatriya by profession or as per his duties. From the events associated with his life, we learn that he himself faced social injustices and fought with the Vedic gods to protect his people from their arrogance.

Dharma Shastras, such as Manusmriti, which were composed much later than the Vedas, sealed whatever chance there was for the caste system to remain flexible. One of the greatest books of social and religious laws ever written in the ancient history of Hinduism, Manusmriti elaborately dwelt upon the various aspects of human conduct and religious life. With its unflinching emphasis on the Dharma and hereditary Varna System, it firmly established the supremacy of the Brahmanas and their exclusive and unquestionable right to perform all religious rites. It firmly declares, "The very birth of a Brahmana is the eternal incarnation of Dharma. For he is born for the sake of Dharma and tends towards becoming one with Brahman." The hereditary caste system precluded large sections of people from utilizing their potential and skills and realizing their dreams. It stifled the creative and intellectual growth of the deprived classes and harmed society in general for a long time. It also forced India's civilization and culture to progress in a narrow channel according to the vision and interests of a few classes whose primary focus was to preserve and promote their interests and privileges rather than the happiness of all.

It is difficult to state how the hereditary caste system, as it is known to us today, took shape on Indian soil and grew in complexity. Today's caste system does not contain just the original four divisions but hundreds and thousands of castes and sub-castes. In all probability, foreign invasions, migration of people from outside, intermixture of castes due to inter-caste marriages, and assimilation of existing tribes and outlier communities must have led to compromises within the system and diversification of castes and caste affiliations. Bactrian Greeks, Huns, Sakas, Kushanas, Chinese, and many others came to India as conquerors, traders, skilled workers, soldiers, artisans, etc. They gradually integrated into the native communities and social practices and adapted their ways, resulting in the formation of a complex social structure consisting of numerous castes.

Whatever the process, the caste system helped the Vedic society grow in complexity without losing its stability or continuity. While the higher castes and those closer to the ruling families enjoyed many privileges, the lower castes suffered from many disabilities and caste discrimination. Especially, the condition of the outcastes (Chandalas) and those belonging to the lower rungs of Shudras was worse. For these unfortunate souls, it mattered little who came and went, who won and lost, who ruled them and did not since their plight remained the same. As long as they submitted to the system, followed the restrictions and injunctions imposed upon them obediently, and paid their taxes or did their unpleasant duties sincerely, they were spared from punishments and ill-treatment. It mattered little to them who sat on the throne and what virtues or vices, or for that matter, what religions or rules their rulers practiced or promoted.

The kings practiced religious tolerance and were benevolent to their subjects. They gave land grants and costly gifts to those they favored, encouraged cultural activities and religious debates and discussions, promoted Dharma, built temples, and patronized art and literature. However, it is doubtful how many regarded the outcasts and lower castes as their subjects, tried to find out their plight, or thought of improving their living conditions. They might have recruited some Shudras for their armies, making provisions for violating the caste rules while segregating their army units on caste lines. Amidst all the churning, political turmoil, and succession of rulers, the outcasts lived rather ignominious lives. Reduced to penury and the lowest social status, oppressed by the political system in which they had no chance of participation, and condemned by the religion that eluded them, they submitted to the unfair conditions life or fate handed them. They worshipped whatever their limited wisdom suggested: rivers, trees, plants, earth, sky, spirits, ancestors, ghosts, demons, and village deities. Some perhaps resorted to crime, magic, and sorcery, doubling as thieves and dacoits or assisting those who indulged in them whenever an opportunity arose. It is difficult to believe that Buddhism gave them any relief since it was not a religion for the weak-minded. It demanded inner purity and observation of the eightfold path, which was difficult to practice even by the strong-willed.

The rulers paid little attention to their subjects except those who were in their service, filled their coffers, served their interests, or with whom they interacted frequently. If they were practicing Vedism, they might have given some importance to the higher castes, especially to those who possessed exceptional knowledge and skills in various arts, crafts, or other fields or served them in some capacity. It is doubtful how far the lower castes mattered to them at all unless they served them in some way. For them, their welfare must have been one of the least considerations in matters of governance since it offered them little advantage or benefit. In theory, these people were condemned by their past, by tradition, by scriptures, and by the inexorable law of karma to lead miserable lives and suffer from the consequences of their sinful past. That was reason enough for the rulers and the higher castes to leave them to their fate. Preoccupied with their own problems of governance, occupational hazards, and survival, always feeling insecure and anxious about their fortunes and the uncertainties of life amid hostilities and palace intrigues, the rulers and their close confidants seldom ventured outside into the outlying areas of their territories and interacted with common people or the less privileged castes. Though theoretically, kings were supposed to care for the welfare of their subjects and treat all their subjects equally and fairly, with a few exceptions here and there, it is hard to believe that they showered their benevolence upon their poor subjects or tried to remove the stigma associated with their castes.

We also have reasons to believe that the hereditary caste system had its limitations and might not have been followed uniformly as dictated by the law books. Strangely, in India's long history, many rulers who ruled in India have been neither Brahmanas nor Kshatriyas but came from lower castes or mixed castes. The same was the case with many seers and saints whom Hindus venerate today. For example, most of the dynasties that ruled from Magadha belonged to lower castes. Yet, they did not seem to have done much to improve the lot of the outcastes and lower castes or made any determined effort to remove caste discrimination or improve their living conditions. The Mauryan emperor, Ashoka, engaged in many welfare activities after he converted to Buddhism, such as building roads, planting trees, and constructing rest houses for travelers. However, we have no evidence to believe that he was sympathetic to the cause of the lower castes or did anything to remove the stigma associated with the outcasts. Most of the rulers hardly cared for anyone's welfare, let alone the outcasts. When they went out to fight wars with their enemies or conquer new territories, accompanied by large armies, the villages through which they passed had to provide them with food, cattle, bullock carts, and other provisions to save themselves from retaliation. It must have put an enormous burden upon the poor agrarian communities, considering that most of them subsisted on meager incomes and had limited resources to support themselves and their families during famines or other natural calamities.

It is indeed difficult to generalize Hindu society on any particular issue since it has always consisted of diverse groups and communities who have practiced many variants of Hinduism since ancient times. The hereditary caste system is no exception. Over the centuries, the Hindu community has also undergone many changes, just like Hinduism. However, the caste system, despite the fact that it underwent many changes, has remained one of its constant and unique features. Despite its drawbacks, it helped people survive and preserve their family names, lineages, traditions, and cultural practices in adverse situations. At the same time, it weakened the community, dividing people on caste and cultural lines and allowing outsiders to exploit and take advantage of them and their internal divisions. It also exposed the subcontinent to numerous foreign invasions on an unprecedented scale in world history.

In the South, the position was slightly different. Here, the fourfold Varna system did not take deep roots. Instead, a hereditary caste system consisting of multiple castes came into existence whose relative importance and status depended upon their political and economic status. The rulers, such as the Satavahanas, Cholas, Chalukyas, Pallavas, Rashtrakutas, Yadavas, Senas, Sakas, Palas, etc., belonged to different castes. Caste divisions existed, but the lower castes and outcasts were not completely excluded from economic activities since their services were needed to keep their homes and fields free from pestilence, predators, and infestations. They also served in the armies and helped their kings win wars. With unity and social cohesion among the Hindus, the South remained largely peaceful and free from foreign invasions. Historically, northern emperors, whether they were Hindus or Muslims, barely managed to rule their southern provinces. Ashoka's empire extended to the edges of Andhra and Karnataka. Yet, it is doubtful how far he managed to rule the territories beyond the Vindhyas. Samudra Gupta led a successful expedition into the South and defeated many rulers of Andhra and Odisha but did not achieve much beyond holding titular titles and collecting taxes. Harshavardhana was defeated and stopped by Pulakesin II on the banks of the river Narmada. Thus, the South, where people practiced Buddhism, Jainism, and Shaivism, which were averse to caste discrimination, remained relatively free from the adverse influences of the rigid caste system practiced in the North.

In contrast to the northern rulers, who never ventured outside the Indian subcontinent, the southern rulers crossed the Bay of Bengal by large fleets of ships and established new kingdoms in the Far East. In countries like Cambodia and Indonesia, we can still discern Hinduism's social, cultural, and religious influence on their people. The South remained largely free from the social and political influences of the North in the medieval period after the formation of the Delhi Sultanate (1206-1526 CE) and the Mughal Empire (1526-1857 CE). Their rulers did invade the South sporadically but left the taxation and administrative matters mostly to the provincial rulers. Many Hindu temples, unlike those in the North, escaped destruction in their hands and stand testimony to the survival and continuity of

Hinduism and its culture in the South. At the same time, Hinduism prospered as the southern rulers built many magnificent temples, some of which have survived until now.

The major takeaway from all this is that Hinduism has better chances to survive and continue if unity and social cohesion prevail among Hindus and if all classes and castes are treated with respect and empathy as a part of God's universal family. That would also increase the chances of more people joining it and the prospects of Hinduism becoming a truly global religion that recognizes humanity, equality, and fraternity as its defining aspects. If Hinduism has to survive as a major world religion and if Hindus want to stand out as an all-inclusive community on the global scene, the hereditary caste system must yield to a more egalitarian and inclusive social system that recognizes class distinctions as an expression of Nature's diversity along with the right of its practitioners to pursue their dreams and desires according to their choices and inclinations and connect to God at the most personal and devotional level through righteousness. The tradition can still acknowledge the existence of four classes of humans as determined by their occupations and professional choices rather than by their birth, heredity, or ancestry.

The hereditary caste system is a human invention and has no justification other than what the Dharma Shastras claim. These Shastras reflect the values and beliefs of bygone eras. When they were formulated, they probably had a valid reason and purpose to justify and promote it in their attempt to preserve and uphold the Dharma and ensure its survival and continuity in difficult times. In the current situation, it is a chief weakness of Hinduism and will remain so if people keep supporting it and vested interests keep taking advantage of it. Those who are interested in the future of Hinduism should stop justifying or rationalizing it since nothing good can be expected of it in an egalitarian society bound to constitutional laws.

The hereditary caste system must give way to a new social order based on the principles of equality and fraternity, where a person's status is determined not by caste but by that person's achievements and character. Hinduism must accommodate people of all backgrounds and allow them to live in harmony and peace so that they exemplify the belief that humanity and all living beings belong to one universal and divine family. It is not a curse to be born in adverse circumstances or belong to a humble social background. Hinduism teaches that before they reenter the mortal world to take another birth, the embodied souls choose their families and circumstances in which they want to take birth. If it is true, some spiritually advanced souls may purposely choose adverse circumstances for their spiritual progress. Therefore, karma need not necessarily be the sole reason for a person's birth or inferior status.

If Hindus do not give up the hereditary caste system in its present form, they cannot blame others for their disunity and disharmony or the increasing number of conversions. They cannot blame foreign interference, charitable institutions, missionary activities, and proselytization for the alienation of these people. They must remember that if there is one force that can weaken or destroy their faith or reduce it to a minority faith on a global scale, it will be the unjust and unfair hereditary caste system.

How Tradition Justified Class Distinctions

Numerous scholars have rationalized the caste system, a significant aspect of ancient Indian society, on various grounds. Those belonging to the higher castes tend to justify it as if it is a perfect system and necessary for the order and regularity of the world, while others hold the opposite opinion and feel that the privileged castes have crafted it to preclude them from social and economic benefits and prevent them from actualizing their dreams and desires. They think that it is an unjust system that must be eradicated so that they can live freely without being singled out for social or economic injustice or mass discrimination. Understanding the justifications for the rather unjust hereditary caste system is crucial to comprehending its historical context in ancient India and how it still survives in Hinduism as the vestigial legacy of its distant past, like a wound that refuses to heal. In this chapter, we will discuss how the heredity caste system, which originally began as a social system based on the distinctions in human nature and personality types and evolved into a rigid, hereditary system, was justified or rationalized in the past and even today, quoting the authority of the scriptures and ascribing to it the sanctity of the divine law or injunction.

Justification in the Vedas

The Vedic tradition recognized the Vedas as the ultimate authority on everything, holding them to be divine and inviolable. If the Vedas confirm that something is true, it must be true, no matter what others think, believe, or say. In other words, no practice, principle, or philosophy is considered valid by the Vedic tradition unless it is found in the Vedas or affirmed by those who excel in their knowledge of them. This principle has served the caste system very well for the last two or three millenniums. Indeed, it would not have thrived or found its approval and universal acceptance in the Vedic world without a clear and indisputable validation by the Vedas. The Purusha Sukta found in the 10th Mandala of the Rigveda describes how the four castes came into existence from different parts of Purusha, the Cosmic Being or Creator, at the time of a grand sacrifice hosted by him with the help of ancient gods serving as the priests [12]. During that sacrifice, in which he used parts of his own body as the offerings, Brahmanas came out of his mouth, Kshatriyas from his arms, Vaisyas from his thighs, and Sudras from his feet. The hymn justified the caste distinctions, or, rather, the scholars used its symbolism to justify the caste distinctions and their relative importance and status in God's creation.

Many scholars believe that the concepts and the imagery of the Purusha Sukta [12] belong to the later Vedic period rather than the Rigvedic period. Hence, it was probably a subsequent interpolation or invention to justify it. Interestingly, this hymn has been quoted by several scholars in the past and today to find virtues in it despite the problems, injustices, and suffering it has caused for so many people and so many generations. We may take the Purusha Sukta as a symbolic interpretation but not literally since the Cosmic Purusha is a being made of pure sattva, devoid of any impurity. Therefore, even if we interpret the hymn literally, it makes no sense. All his bodily parts must be equally pure and divine and worthy of worship. Indeed, in devotional traditions, it is customary for devotees to worship His feet rather than any other part of his body. Therefore, if God's feet are worthy of worship, why should those who are born from it be considered inferior or unworthy of knowing the Vedas?

Justification in the theory of Karma

The hereditary caste system is validated by the karma doctrine, according to which each person's previous actions (karma) determine that person's present and future. This chain of events arising from one's karma continues over several lives. Good deeds lead to an auspicious future, and evil deeds lead to an inauspicious future. Good deeds lead to heavenly life or liberation, and evil deeds lead to hell or a life of suffering and rebirth as an inferior jiva. The Bhagavadgita[13] clearly states that those who uphold Dharma and perform their obligatory duties sincerely are born into a family of pious people amid favorable circumstances in their next birth. Thus, the karma doctrine favors the idea that those who are born into lower castes or adverse circumstances have no one but themselves to blame for their suffering. Their pitiable plight is a warning to others that the wheel of Dharma operates inexorably, sparing none and favoring none. If someone is born as an outcast or with social and economic disadvantages, it must be because they must have committed serious offenses in their past lives. Their present lives must be an opportunity to remedy that and improve their chances of attaining a good birth in their next lives.

The scriptures, including the Bhagavadgita and many Upanishads, support this line of argument. According to them, people must live righteously, with self-restraint, renunciation, and detachment, worship God with devotion, and offer their actions to God without desires as a sacrifice to escape from karma and attain liberation. The Bhagavadgita warns that those who engage in sinful actions will be cast to sinful wombs. In the fourth chapter of the book, Lord Krishna declares that he created the fourfold Varna system according to a jiva's karma and essential nature [13]. By combining karma doctrine with the caste system and one's essential nature, the ancient lawmakers prescribed different vocational and occupational duties and obligations for each caste. They expect people to follow them strictly and perform their obligatory duties as ordained by them. Observing them without questioning them or ignoring them is an act of merit, which entitles them to progress spiritually and obtain a better life in their next lives [14].

The connection between a person's karma and his rebirth cannot be questioned. However, the hereditary caste system ignores the fact that apart from fate or acts of God, self-willed or self-induced actions also play an important role in shaping a person's future and destiny. Without caste limitations, people will have better opportunities to resolve their karma and improve their living conditions. People must have the freedom to make decisions and choose their actions so that they will have better opportunities to resolve their karma and make further spiritual progress.

Justification on the basis of the triple Gunas

Hinduism firmly believes that all the diversity of Nature (Prakriti) arises from 24 primordial forms (tattvas) and three modes (gunas). Their permutations and combinations are responsible for the diversity of names and forms (nama rupa) and their characteristics. The gunas are also responsible for the essential nature (prakriti svabhavam) of each jiva. Their expression or suppression in the jivas causes them to act in specific ways and makes themselves suitable or unsuitable for certain situations, possibilities, behaviors, and functions. The same logic holds for all humans also. The three modes are Sattva, Rajas, and Tamas. Sattva is characterized by purity and spirituality and manifests in humans as the propensity for truthfulness, knowledge, intelligence, faith, sincerity, devotion, gentleness, and so on. Sattva is believed to be the predominant mode of those who engage in spiritual practices, pursue divine knowledge and live virtuously. The Brahmanas are supposed to be predominantly sattvic and, thereby, pure and pious.

The mode of rajas characterizes passions, egoism, pride, and worldliness. It is present predominantly in those who are restless and driven by passions, desires, and attachments. They engage in actions to assert themselves. Tamas is the third mode. It is responsible for dark desires and passions, delusion, ignorance, and extreme nature. People in whom it is present predominantly are characterized by lethargy, intoxication, perversion, extreme thinking, and disregard for tradition and established norms. It manifests in humans as ignorance, lack of ambition, extreme nature, imprudence, demonical resolve, uncleanliness, negativity, uncleanliness, unhealthy habits, and antisocial behavior. Rajas, followed by sattva and tamas, are said to be responsible for the characteristic nature of the Vaishyas. Tamas is believed to be the predominant mode of those who are driven by baser desires and instinct lack discernment, and act irrationally. These characteristics are believed to be characteristic of the Shudras.

While the modes are responsible for the essential nature of the jivas and their actions, it is incorrect to justify the hereditary caste system based on that. There is no guarantee that a sattvic child will be born to sattvic parents or a rajasic one to rajasic parents. Apart from genetics, environmental factors also influence a person's nature and behavior. For example, Prahlada, a pious devotee of Lord Vishnu, was born to a tamasic demon name Hiranya Kasipu. Many pious souls, such as Valmiki and Vyasa, were not born as Brahmanas but earned great distinction as seers and exemplified the Brahmana nature. In other words, a person's essential nature does not necessarily arise from birth but from that person's self-effort.

Justification by religious laws

As we have stated before, the Dharma Shastras are essentially treatises about the Hindu caste system and how people should behave and fulfill their obligations to themselves, to others, and to God according to their castes and caste-based occupations. Manusmriti (1.88) states that to protect this universe, the glorious God created and assigned separate duties and occupations to the four varnas who sprang from his mouth, arms, thighs, and feet, respectively. Whoever performs such duties selflessly will reach the immortal state and attain all the desires he ever wished to attain. Thus, the Hindu lawbooks (Dharmashastras) unequivocally approve the caste system and formulate their laws regarding moral and religious duties, obligations, values, character, ethical conduct, punishments, etc., accordingly. They have no problem discriminating against people according to their castes and suggesting different value systems for each. They prescribe different rules and disciplinary measures for their conduct, religious duties, and punishments. They not only justify a rigid, hereditary caste system but prescribe lenient punishments for higher castes and severe punishments for the lower castes for the same unlawful conduct.

They do declare that a person becomes a Brahmana by exemplary behavior but do not confer any distinction or special status on those who are not Brahmanas or Kshatriyas by birth but exemplify virtuous conduct befitting them. We do not know how extensive their influence was or how sincerely their laws and injunctions were implemented in ancient times. We may presume that they were followed mostly where the Brahmana influence prevailed and where the rulers took upon themselves the duties of upholding and enforcing them as the protectors of Dharma. Probably even in such cases, their reach was limited to a few higher castes. If the kings practiced other religions or followed different laws, probably these laws were never promulgated except in areas where the local village councils (panchayats) practiced Hinduism and relied upon their knowledge of the law books to settle disputes or dispense justice.

Critical Analysis

The Hindu caste system had its own merits and demerits and should not be judged purely based on the moral and social values of today. Inequalities and social divisions based on economic and family status were not unknown in other parts of the world or other civilizations. The Nordic races followed some form of caste system. The Greeks and Romans of the ancient world had a class system consisting of freemen and enslaved people. The Persians also had a social and political hierarchy, which was conveniently exploited by Alexander when he invaded the Persian empire. The British, the French, and the Russians had their landed gentry and nobility in contrast to the commoners and peasants, who were subject to discriminatory taxation laws and unequal and unfair treatment. The New World, founded by conquests and mass immigration from Europe, had its enslaved classes and its highly discriminatory class system that was practiced for nearly two centuries propped up and legitimized by unjust laws. Compared to some of these institutions and practices, the Hindu caste system was more humane and benign.

Although the outcastes (chandalas) were treated with contempt and excluded from social interaction, communication, and participation in religious activities, they were free within their bubble to practice their vocations and follow their laws. So was the case with the groups identified by the tradition as the Sudras. The fear of sin and karma kept the higher castes from treating them cruelly or unjustly, although they favored discrimination and allowed the unjust system to prevail. Similar factors allowed the deprived classes to put up with the system and allowed themselves to settle for a life of suffering and social inequality.

The Romans had their slave revolts. The French had their revolution of the proletariat and the deprived classes. The Russians had their socialist revolution supported by the serfs and factory workers. The injustices of the American slave system produced deep-rooted divisions, resentment, aggression, and frustration in the USA among those who endured it and their descendants. In contrast, the outcastes and low castes of India did not launch armed rebellions or large-scale organized revolts or indulged in violence against the upper castes who either oppressed them or allowed the injustices to continue with their tacit indifference. The caste system upheld social and economic inequalities but did not approve of unwarranted violence or cruelty toward the oppressed castes. With the help of discriminatory and restrictive laws and by invoking divine and scriptural authority, the system limited their opportunities to pursue their goals, practice their faith, exercise their freedom, or work for their betterment. They created rigid walls around them and kept them within their confines, bound to the authority of religious institutions and fear of retribution and divine punishment. However, within those walls, life went on as usual, independent of how others lived. The hereditary caste system might have had its justification in the past, but today, certainly, it does not have any justification to continue and does not make many people feel proud of their caste or social background.

Varna, Dharma, and Varnashrama Dharma

Hinduism is not an organized religion. There are no specific institutions that govern the lives and the conduct of its followers. In such circumstances, how best can Hindus practice their faith and uphold their Dharma? In Hinduism, families provide the best guidance. Hindus learn about their faith primarily from their parents and elders in their families. From them and by observing them, they come to know about their family traditions, beliefs and practices, deities, and methods of worship. They may learn some aspects of it on their own by studying the scriptures, observing others, or from their own experience and exploration. They may also learn by visiting temples and interacting with priests, elders, and others in the community.

In Hinduism, self-study (svadhyaya) or self-effort plays an important role. Many people become acquainted with their religious beliefs and practices through self-study, analysis, and self-learning. In the modern age, the Internet has become a significant source of information about almost every aspect of religion, including Hinduism. It provides access to scriptures, scholarly articles, and discussions, which can be an important source for self-study, learning, and mastery. In Hinduism, belief in the karma doctrine is also important. It suggests how karma or desire-ridden actions leave a cumulative effect on the lives and destinies of people and influence their past and future lives. Hindus believe that just as karma shapes our lives, it also determines their essential nature, which in turn influences their beliefs, practices, and natural propensities that determine the gods they worship and the methods and paths they choose to practice their faith and pursue liberation.

The Vedic Varna system is deeply rooted in the concept of Dharma, which primarily means religious or moral obligatory duty. The scriptures identified all the duties necessary to ensure the orderly progression of the world. They divided them into four or five categories and assigned them to different groups. Thus, the four varnas came into existence. The scriptures, especially the Dharma

Shastras (law books), ordained that each class of people must perform their obligatory duty, failing which they would fail to attain heaven and suffer in hell or will take birth in the bodies of lower life forms. That was warning enough in the ancient days for people to stick to their obligatory duties and avoid sinful consequences. The Varna system became rigid and hereditary to ensure that people learned about their duties from an early age and passed their knowledge of them and the skills associated with them to the next generation without any delay or confusion. If it were not hereditary, it would have been very difficult to ensure the continuation of the Dharma or set of obligatory duties pertaining to each Varna. The rigid and hereditary caste system ensured the continuation of Hinduism and its numerous and complex ritual and spiritual practices through difficult phases of history. Thus, the idea of Dharma not only gave birth to the varnas but also ensured its continuity despite its drawbacks. History is proof that it served its aims and ensured that Hinduism remains, until now, the world's oldest living and continuing religion or Dharma.

One's journey to Hinduism is often unique and deeply personal. At a young age, people may not pay much attention to religious matters. However, as they grow, at some point, they may turn to their faith due to past life impressions (samskaras) or predominant inclinations to find solace or find answers to their problems. Chance meetings with spiritual people, adversity, problems, and difficulties may also push one toward their faith. Sometimes, people emerge through grave situations, accidents, severe illnesses, and near-death experiences, which may teach them the value of life and the importance of leading a spiritual life. This emphasis on personal experiences in Hinduism fosters a sense of individuality and uniqueness in one's spiritual journey.

Without a rigid social system and well-defined duties and social responsibilities for each group, without attributing them to the divine authority or validation by the scriptures, and without invoking the fear of divine retribution or sinful consequences, people may not care to fulfill their obligations or take them seriously. If they neglect their duties, it could lead to the decline of Dharma and people's commitment to its teachings, beliefs, and practices, resulting in confusion, disorder, and the rise of immorality and irreligiosity (adharma). The hereditary caste system took care of this problem by entrusting the authority to the upper castes. They played a crucial role in protecting and upholding Dharma and ensuring its survival and continuity even when they lacked political or institutional authority to enforce the system and even when the majority of people did not know the scriptures, their duties, or the rules and restraints prescribed by the law books. However, the caste system also had a negative side, as it precluded many from participating in the more essential duties that are necessary for establishing an egalitarian and inclusive society. We have already discussed the downside of the caste system and how it has affected many classes of people for centuries. Despite its drawbacks, the caste system's historical significance in preserving Hinduism cannot be overlooked.

The connection between Varna and Dharma can be understood from the fact that the Hindu law books, called the Dharma Shastras, exclusively and extensively deal with the laws pertaining to each Varna. They identify the four varnas, ascribe different duties and codes of conduct to each of them, and distinguish them from those who are outside the system since they perform different duties and follow a different code of conduct that is outside the scope of the Varna system. They prescribe four chief aims of human life for the householders of the three upper castes, which they must pursue during the four phases or ashramas of life by performing the obligatory duties that are specific to each ashrama.

The four purusharthas

The chief aims are known as the Purusharthas, or purposes or reasons (arthas) for which the embodied souls (Purushas) must live. The Vedas identify four of them, namely Dharma, Artha, Kama, and Moksha, the last one being the highest and the ultimate aim of all. Dharma refers to the practice of Dharma, which involves studying and reciting the scriptures to acquire the right knowledge, performing sacrificial duties and sacraments (samskaras) that are declared obligatory by the Vedas, and living righteously following the approved and prescribed code of conduct specific to each varna.

Artha involves the pursuit of earning wealth righteously and living righteously according to the injunctions of the Vedas and the moral and ethical laws prescribed by the scriptures. The wealth earned must be spent on righteous causes and for performing obligatory duties to uphold Dharma and ensure the order and regularity of the world. Kama means either sexual desire or desire in general. Householders must pursue such desires to obtain progeny and ensure the transmigration of their ancestors and the continuity of their family lineages. Selfish desires lead to sin and suffering. Selfless desires lead to peace, happiness, and liberation. Moksha, or liberation from the cycle of births and deaths (samsara), is the ultimate aim. If the Dharma is the foundation, Artha and Kama are the means, and Moksha is the true goal (paramartha). All the four aims are interconnected, emphasizing the holistic nature of Hinduism. The pursuit of one goal should not negate, contradict, or hinder any of the other three.

The Varnashrama Dharma

The law books also identify the four phases of human life through the householders belonging to the three upper castes must pass through to attain liberation or heavenly life. They are Brahmacharya, Grihasta, Vanaprastha and Sannyasa.

Brahmacharya

Brahmacharya is meant for students and young children who are initiated into Vedic education or for those who have given up worldly life and are engaged in ascetic practices. In this phase, students of the Vedas must focus on their education under the care of a guru or their parents, practice self-control and discipline and live austerely according to a strict code of conduct, practicing celibacy. They must pursue Dharma, practice self-control, serve their teachers, and live righteously according to the principles of Dharma. Since celibacy is vital in this phase, it is called Brahmacharya, the observance of celibacy or the worship of Brahma. The law books prescribe several rules for them, such as when and where they should bathe, what they should do when going out to beg for food, how they should avoid contact with women, and how they should serve their teachers.

Grihasta

In the next phase, called Grihasta, the young adult who has completed his education must marry a suitable bride to perform his obligatory duties as a householder. Manu (3.2) says that those who complete their education (the study of one or more Vedas) without breaking the code of conduct prescribed for them are qualified to enter the order of Grihasta. In this phase, he must pursue the triple aims of Dharma, Artha and Kama, with an eye to the ultimate aim of Moksha. They must perform daily sacrifices (nitya karmas), occasional sacrifices, sacraments, and other duties to ensure their welfare and the welfare of the world. They must nourish gods, ancestors, seers, sages, and others through sacrifices. Indeed, this phase is crucial since their actions in this phase determine their karma, fate, and rebirth. A householder, by the very nature of his duties, cannot escape from sinful conduct or causing suffering to others. Therefore, as a remedy and expiation, they must perform daily sacrifices.

Vanaprastha

The next phase is called Vanaprastha, or the way of the forest. A householder may enter this phase after completing his obligatory duties and fulfilling his responsibilities towards his family, gods, and ancestors or at any time he wishes to do so. According to today's standards, this corresponds to the retirement age. In this phase, householders who have given up their active duties must retire to forests or secluded places and prepare themselves for the harsh life of sannyasa, the fourth phase. They must live simple lives like hermits in secluded places and spend their time in study, contemplation, expiation, purification, self-control, detachment, and other spiritual practices, sleeping on the floor and giving up all luxuries, comforts, and worldly delights. According to Gautama, they should not possess any wealth, live by seeking alms, give up all desires, and wear simple clothes to cover their nakedness. Manu says that when a householder sees that his skin is wrinkled, his hair is white, and that his children have children, he may retire to a forest, with or without his wife, and abandon all food produced from cultivation. He should still perform his daily sacrifices with roots, herbs, fruit, etc. Whatever the specific actions they perform, they should utilize this time to cultivate dispassion, stability, detachment, and sameness, practicing self-control and self-purification.

Sannyasa

The final phase of life is sannyasa. In this phase, they must give up everything, including eating cooked food, and subsist entirely on natural food discarded by trees and plants, having become tired of obtaining food through begging. He must become indifferent to everything, determined to achieve liberation, establishing his mind in the contemplation of Brahman. According to Vashista, they must practice nonviolence, live in peace with everyone, and give up performing all religious ceremonies and sacrifices. According to Manu, in the fourth part of his life, the householder must live as an ascetic, abandoning all attachments to worldly objects. He must give up making fire, cooking food, staying in sheltered places, and wandering from place to place. He should desire neither to live nor to die but wait for his final departure. He should become pure and harmless in thought and deed, bear suffering, insult no one, and take delight in the Self.

Nowadays, hardly anyone practices their obligatory duties or follows the Varnashrama Dharma as ordained by the Vedas or prescribed by the Dharma Shastras. However, many Hindus practice domestic worship (puja), make offerings to gods, and occasionally perform sacraments, penances (vratas), and sacrifices on important occasions. They also celebrate festivals, visit temples, and go on pilgrimages. Hinduism also has a long history of ascetic movements and traditions mostly associated with the sectarian traditions of Shaivism and Vaishnavism. People in old age may turn to spirituality, but it is not a universal practice. The facts, Dharma is not practiced with the same sincerity and determination as the Vedic people used to practice. Of the four phases of human life, the most popular one is the Grihasta. Except for those who have taken the vows of sannyasa or renounced worldly, hardly anyone practices the five restraints: nonviolence, truthfulness, non-stealing, abstinence, and non-possessiveness.

The Caste System in Ascetic Traditions

The caste system or the division of the varnas forced Vedic householders in ancient times to perform their obligatory duties, even if they were difficult or economically expensive, with the fear of divine retribution and sinful karma looming over them. At the same time, the system and the scriptures compensated for those burdensome tasks with social and economic privileges in proportion to the degree of importance their duties carried. The varnas were meant to create a viable social order and regulate people's lives. In establishing it, its originators did not intend to create social inequalities or injustices, or they might have thought that it was inevitable due to the play of Maya and karma. Whatever the truth may be, the caste or the varna system applied to people who practiced the Vedic Dharma. Even among them, caste rules and duties were applicable only to those who were willing to take on the duties of householders. It is possible even among them, some might have neglected or ignored their duties, taking responsibility for their actions or rationalizing them according to their convenience.

Besides, the obligatory duties and the laws associated with them were not applicable, as is the customary practice even today, to those who renounced worldly life or abandoned Dharma and converted to another religion or belief system. For the faithful, the varnas and the duties associated with each of them carried great weight in worldly life and formed the basis for their transmigration, destinies, and the continuation of their fortunes and family lineages. The seers who established them and designated the duties for each Varna did not intend to make them the sole purpose of human life. They understood that everyone would not be inclined to perform obligatory duties as householders or pursue the four aims of human life. Some might be born, due to past life karma, with an uncontrollable aspiration to pursue liberation and avoid the first three phases of human life: Brahmacharya, Grihasta, and Vanaprastha. Therefore, they prescribed the norms only to those who willingly became householders and performed the duties associated with their varnas. Those who renounced worldly life and pursued liberation by becoming ascetics (sannyasis) were excluded from the compulsion to perform them.

Indeed, as we discussed before, the Hindu Varnashrama Dharma is the dharma of all dharmas. It lays down rules and duties that people must follow in each phase of their lives, starting from their initiation and beginning as students. As students, they must study relevant texts and acquire the knowledge necessary to perform their duties; as adults, they must perform their household duties pursuing the four chief aims: Dharma, Artha, Kama, and Moksha; after fulfilling their obligations, they retire from active duty and live like hermits or recluses, giving up desires and attachments, reflecting upon the deeper aspects of life, contemplating upon God and cultivating detachment and devotion. In the final phase of life, they must renounce everything, become homeless, wandering ascetics (a sanyasi), and pursue liberation with single-minded determination. In brief, this was the blueprint of life prescribed by the Vedas for all castes. However, there is no compulsion that everyone must follow this pattern. People can take up sannyasa at any time in their lives, giving up their duties, desires, and attachments to engage in the spiritual sacrifice of liberation. Sannyasa is the highest and the ultimate sacrifice since it requires the sacrifice of everything, including the longing for life and all willful and desire-ridden actions. They must also sacrifice all the identities arising from their names, last names, families, castes, associations, duties, and professions. In short, they must live as Shudras, with humility, and without ego, as if they have no standing in life.

Rules for recluses and ascetics

When we study the rulers pertaining to each Varna or caste in the context of the Varnashrama Dharma, we can see that obligatory duties and varnas are relevant only in the first two stages of human life. They become irrelevant once householders retire from their active duties and resort to the life of a hermit or a recluse (vanaprastha). They may still have duties and obligations in the third and fourth phases of their lives, but they are no longer considered a part of the castes or families into which they are born unless they continue to live with their families and engage in running their households directly or indirectly. The idea is that those who want to take up sannyasa must be willing to break away from their past and sever all connections so that they can begin a new journey and new life, unburdened by their past. They must also avoid all connections with worldly people and avoid visiting places where they live except when they go out for food. Even on such occasions, they are bound by several rules and restraints and must remain guarded.

The law books are clear on this. For example, Vasistha stipulates that those who retire to forests and dwell in the forests as hermits or recluses should not enter any village or step on plowed land. They should remain chaste, their hearts full of meekness, honoring the guests who visit them irrespective of their caste or background, giving whatever they have, and not receiving anything in return. They must observe cleanliness, taking three baths a day. Thus, discharging their duties towards everyone, they must attain self-control and equanimity.

Bauddhayana distinguishes two kinds of hermits: those who cook food and those who do not. Both are meant to observe a strict code of conduct to gain control over their minds and bodies but are free from the duties and obligations meant for the householders of their varnas. Gautama stipulates that hermits who retire from active duties should live in a forest subsisting on roots and fruits, practicing austerities. They may still offer oblations by kindling fire and worship gods, ancestors, celestial beings, and seers but must subsist on wild-growing vegetables only. They may also receive the hospitality of people of all castes except those with whom intercourse is forbidden. They may even consume the flesh of animals killed by beasts to keep their bodies alive since that does not violate their practice of nonviolence. In other words, they should renounce caste identities and caste-based distinctions and live religiously, subsisting on a meager diet, avoiding social contacts, and practicing rules and restraints that are necessary for their purification and transformation.

The law books further state that in the fourth phase of their lives as ascetics (sannyasis), which is difficult and painful, they must practice renunciation to perfection, giving up everything, including their first and last names, family and caste identities, desires, and attachments, food choices, comforts, and luxuries. They must give up everything connected to their past, leaving no mark or trace of who they were or the caste to which they belonged. They are even supposed to give up wearing the sacred thread. In the Jabala Upanishad, Yajnavalkya explains to Atri why this is important. He says, "This (Self) alone is the sacred thread of him who purifies himself by offering and sipping water. This is the ordained method (vidhi) for the Parivrajakas, the ascetics, who have renounced worldly life." Thus, in the Vedic times, the wandering ascetics were prohibited from wearing caste marks, betraying any visible sign of caste affiliations, or showing preference for particular castes. They were also prohibited from possessing anything, living in the same house or at the same for long except during rains, avoiding entering villages and towns except for begging, and seeking alms only late in the day after people completed eating their midday meals.

To quote from the Jabala Upanishad again, in the following passage, Yajnavalkya describes the ideal life and conduct of the great souls (Paramahansa) who pursue Brahman, mentioning their specific names and how they attained the exalted state of self-realization.

"Here are Samvartaka, Aruni, Svetaketu, Durvasa, Ribhu, Nidagha, Jada-Bharata, Dattatreya, Raivataka, and others who are known by the name Paramahansas. They bear no distinguishing marks, act in mysterious ways, and are free from intoxication but behave as if they are intoxicated. Throwing into the water the three-pronged staff (tridandam), the water jug (kamandalam), the tuft of hair on the back of their heads, the sacred thread, and saying Bhuh Svaha, they (who want to become Paramahansas) should search for the Self. Resorting to the nakedness they had at birth, without any attachments, without holding on to anything, they should follow the path of Brahman. With a pure mind that is endowed with stable intelligence, for the sake of sustaining their breath, with the alms they collect at the appointed times, they should fill the vessel of their stomachs, remaining equal to whether they received the alms or not. They must live in an empty house, a temple, a shelter made of grass or straw, an anthill, the base of a tree, a potter's house, a house where the sacred fire is lit, the sandy bank of a river,

a hill, a cave, a hollow of a tree, a waterfall or a mountain torrent in a deserted place. Without effort, free from egoism, with the mind firmly established in the Self, intent upon ending the consequences of impure actions, they must finally give up their bodies on the path of renunciation. That one who observes all these goes by the name Paramahansa. Indeed, they go by the name Paramahansa."

According to the Vashista Sutras, those who enter the phase of Sannyasa must shun society and public attention and act as if they were out of their minds (10.19). The same principles shall apply in case of their death also. For them, caste-based funeral rites or cremation methods are explicitly prohibited. They must spend the last days of their lives in secluded places or the houses of low-caste people. When they die, they must be buried rather than cremated, or their bodies must be dropped into the waters of a flowing river or left in the open to become food for wild animals. Thus, we can see that the law books leave little scope for confusion. They make sure that recluses and ascetics abandon their caste-related duties and identities fully and break free from their past as householders and their connections with their castes and families.

From the above, we can infer that the caste system is meant to support the householders, helping them serve the world and fulfill their obligations to others, such as the gods, ancestors, humans, and other creatures. It is meant to provide a definitive purpose and structure to their lives and help them serve God as His true representatives on earth. The law books declare the path of the Grihastas (householders) as superior to all other paths, including the path of recluses and ascetics, since it is vital for the continuation of creation and life on earth.

The Pros and Cons of the Caste System

The Hindu caste system was born out of a social necessity to preserve and continue the Vedic way of life and ensure the purity and continuation of the tradition, its knowledge and beliefs, and the family lineages that propagated it and exemplified its ideals. It has many advantages. In the past, it served the purpose for which it was invented: the preservation and continuation of Dharma with inbuilt safeguards and checks and balances. However, unfortunately it also led to many unhealthy social practices and caused a great deal of harm to certain people. In this chapter, we will discuss the advantages and disadvantages of the hereditary caste system that became the defining aspect of Hinduism in the past as well as today.

The Advantages

1. Continuity of traditions: It would be unfair to say that the Hindu caste system had no merit because if it were true, it would not have survived for so long. If Hinduism survived amidst many competing traditions, religions, and foreign invasions, without a central authority and with many centrifugal forces working against it from all directions, a great deal of credit must be given to the rigid caste system that discouraged people from experimenting with their faith and beliefs acting as a binding force and kept them within the boundaries established by the scriptures and the tradition. A vast majority of the Hindus in the ancient world were illiterate. However, they were not ignorant of the laws of karma and the implications of violating caste rules or disregarding their commitment to their caste-based family occupations and their role in ensuring their and their kins' well-being and survival.

2. Division of labor: The caste system, with its division of labor and specialization of knowledge, fostered a unique system of vocational skills. Each family had the opportunity to perfect and improve their skills, passing them down through generations. The elders served as teachers, imparting their knowledge to the younger members, creating a cycle of learning and growth.

3. Bonds of Brotherhood: The caste system fostered the development of caste-based guilds in urban areas, akin to workers' unions and financial and professional institutions. These guilds united people under a common banner with a shared purpose, safeguarding their interests and providing a form of social insurance against unfair competition and unjust exploitation. They ensured fair wages, provided loans, and facilitated employment, promoting work ethics and higher standards of performance. In rural areas, the caste system brought together people of the same caste, fostering understanding and cooperation. It promoted unity, solidarity, and fraternity, strengthening the bonds of their relationships through marriage, friendship, and other forms of social and professional interaction.

4. Purity of lineages: Because of the rigid rules regarding marriage and relations with other castes and the prohibition of marriages within the same gotras, the hereditary caste system helped people maintain the purity of their lineages and allegiances to their ancestry and family traditions. It also helped preserve and reinforce many ancient beliefs and practices and ensured the continuation of Hinduism for millenniums despite foreign invasions and oppressive regimes. Even today, caste is an important factor in fixing marriages or determining the compatibility and suitability of bride and groom. This is true, especially in rural communities where a person's caste determines family status and social image.

5. Unity in diversity: The caste system, at least in theory, was not just about the division of labor or the supply of a committed and loyal workforce. Apart from recognizing inequalities and injustices arising from people's karma, it also emphasized the underlying unity of all the castes, their connection to one source, God himself, and their divine nature as the creations and integral parts of one Universal Being. The system was designed to establish social order, regulate the affairs of the people, and preserve the sacred law (Dharma) based on certain eternal principles and human values. It acknowledged diversity and inequality as the inherent properties of Nature and the role of God as the protector of this order. As His true representatives on earth, it was also the responsibility of human beings to perform their obligatory duties to ensure order and regularity and prevent the world from falling into chaos and unrest due to intermixture and confusion of castes or the ascendence of evil.

Disadvantages

The following are some of the disadvantages of the hereditary caste system.

1. Exploitation of the Weak: The Hindu caste system, with its inherent weaknesses, became unjust and exploitative over time. It gave rise to social injustices, disabilities, and inequalities among a vast majority of people whom it summarily declared as inferior, unfit, and unqualified to live freely and realize their dreams and desires. Its rigidity and oppressive enforcement in the name of God, religion, and tradition exposed the weaker sections of society to unjust exploitation by the socially and politically privileged groups for their own good.

2. Disunity and division of loyalties: The caste system divided Indian society vertically and horizontally into several groups and fostered distrust and resentment. It promoted disunity, divisions, narrowmindedness, and caste prejudices among them and weakened their desire to work together for the common good. The disunity helped outside groups to exploit them.

3. Foreign domination: The caste system and the divisions it fostered and foisted upon the people weakened their resolve to stand united against foreign invasions and oppressive regimes. The able-bodied working class, traditionally designated as Sudras, was condemned to serve the landed gentry, royalty, and the aristocracy as indentured agricultural laborers reserved for manual labor and menial jobs. In another world and time, they could have been employed better in the military and administrative duties to deal with the invading armies and protect them and the faith from threats they posed. By relegating the physically strong population to manual work and subservience and ignoring them in important matters and challenging tasks, the Hindu rulers deprived themselves of a strong physical force to defend themselves and their empires against foreign aggression. It is interesting to note that the Muslim rulers and the Britishers, who occupied India, recruited people of all castes for their military units and, with their help, were able to defeat the local rulers and establish their rule for centuries.

4. Preferential Treatment: The caste system was based on birth and heredity rather than individual talent and vocational choice. This created many disabilities for talented people belonging to the lower castes. The story of Ekalavya in the Mahabharata is a good example of how the system invented and justified a value system and conventional beliefs and practices that protected and guaranteed the interests of privileged classes while leaving the lower castes to fend for themselves and remaining at their mercy. Talented people from the lower strata of society were ignored or sidelined since they either posed a threat to the stability of the social structure and its continuity or were discarded by the system as unfit and unqualified. The discrimination was justified on the grounds of Dharma and God's eternal laws. This biased approach stunted the growth of the nation and contributed to its downfall over time.

5. Political and military implications: The caste system placed foreigners on par with the untouchables and prevented a healthy exchange of knowledge and ideas. Native people loathed the idea of going to foreign lands or crossing the oceans. This worked to the disadvantage of Indians in general and the armies in particular, as it isolated people from the rest of the world and prevented them from knowing about the invading foreigners, their strategic moves and countermoves, and methods of warfare. The caste system also divided Indian soldiers on caste lines and created groups within groups, making coordination a difficult task for the army generals.

6. Conversion to other religions: The caste system indirectly contributed to the decline of Hinduism in certain sections of Hindu society as many people belonging to the lower castes and outcastes were effortlessly converted to other religions by promising social equality and better economic status. Through conversions, the missionaries offered them an easy and convenient escape from centuries of social stigma, indignities, and inequalities associated with their castes and social identities. In many ways, Buddhism, Christianity, and Islam managed to thrive in India mostly because of the weaknesses of Hinduism rather than any religious or spiritual merit they possessed. Speaking of this subject, Swami Vivekananda commented in the following words, "Was there ever a sillier thing before in the world than what I saw in .....? The poor Pariah is not allowed to pass through the same street as the high-caste man, but if he changes his name to a hodge-podge English name, it is all right; or to a Mohammedan name, it is all right. What inference would you draw except that these .... are all lunatics, their homes so many lunatic asylums, and that they are to be treated with derision by every race in India until they mend their manners and know better."

7. Instrument of oppression: The caste system became an instrument of oppression in the hands of socially privileged castes. Landlords and wealthy merchants exploited the lower castes. They subjected them to inhuman treatment without fear, as the lower castes did not enjoy equal rights nor the confidence of those who enforced the laws.

8. Untouchability: The caste system created a class of individuals who were regarded as untouchables and treated as less than human beings. They were not allowed to enter the cities and villages freely. People of higher castes were advised not to touch them or let their shadows fall on them because the shadows were also treated as sources of defilement. They were not allowed to draw water from the wells or ponds used by the upper castes. In modern times, many untouchables converted to other religions because they saw no hope in sticking with their traditional castes. Among those who did not opt for conversion, the educated ones are its worst critics.

9. Low self-esteem: The caste system lowers the self-esteem of many and makes them feel bad about their social status and caste identity. Since it is based on birth, there is nothing much anyone can do about one's caste other than changing one's religion, a decision that may have other social implications, such as alienation from one's own family, friends, or community, accompanied by feelings of guilt and fear of divine retribution. The caste system is a blistering and festering ancient sore of Hindu society that evokes painful memories and keeps the Hindu society divided forever.

The Varna As a Way of Life

Although Hinduism is not an organized religion and has no institutional leadership that can speak for all its followers, regulate their beliefs, practices, and conduct, or resolve their disputes and differences of opinion, its absence is compensated very much by other methods. They are built into the framework of Hinduism and have proven effective in its long history. For example, the caste system, varnashrama dharma, the purusharthas, the concept of sacrifice as a way of life and the foundation of Dharma, methods of worship and spiritual practice, its rich body of ageless literature that still holds its influence on the masses, its thriving ascetic and spiritual traditions that promise to purify, uplift and expand human consciousness and essential nature – these and many more served as guiding factors of the faith over the centuries and through the tumultuous periods of its history. It also has a rich body of right-hand and left-hand ritual and spiritual practices backed by centuries-old scriptures and teaching traditions, which give the devotees many choices and alternatives to pursue their religious and spiritual aspirations according to their knowledge and inclinations. These diverse aspects of Hinduism bear testimony to its rich cultural history, connecting us to our ancient roots and traditions.

These alternatives are integrated into its Varna system, which categorizes people into different groups according to their nature, whereby people with different natures, temperaments, and resolve can practice their Dharma without feeling conflicted or suffering from doubt, confusion, or a crisis of faith. No doubt, in its present form, the caste system has many flaws and is even criticized by many for the problems and divisions it creates for the faith and the community at various levels. However, its original intentions were noble, at least in theory. In the early Vedic period, the Varna system was designed to apportion the various duties among four classes of humans, each representing particular personality traits, natures, drives, aims, and aspirations so that by performing them, they could ensure the orderly progression of the society and the world.

Unfortunately, the system deviated from its intended path and devolved into a hereditary class system, producing unintended consequences, including inequality and social injustice, and negating the very purposes for which it was intended: unity, discipline, order, and harmony.

Despite its flaws, the caste system harbors noble ideas. The most significant of these is the opportunity it offers to ordinary humans to preserve and uphold God's creation by executing His eternal duties as His devoted and trusted servants or representatives on earth. Human beings are crafted in the image of Isvara, the Cosmic Person, to cultivate and manifest His supreme qualities and nature in their conduct and consciousness and His will through their actions without claiming ownership or doership. The caste system offers a platform for humans to execute His duties as their own, without assuming their ownership and doership, and uphold and serve His creation in four distinct ways.

The basis of each caste is the essential nature (svabhavam) of the people who represent it, which is in turn determined by their predominant gunas: sattva, rajas, and tamas. These gunas arise in them from Prakriti (Nature), and each of them produces distinguishable characteristics, personalities, types, likes, dislikes, and behaviors. Sattva represents purity and manifests in us as physical vigor, spiritual illumination, purity, clarity, mental brilliance, gentleness, scholarship, righteousness, etc. The mode of rajas manifests in humans as passion, activity, dynamism, power, change, physical strength, valor, fearlessness, ambition, competitiveness, pride, etc. Tamas represents negative qualities such as ignorance, delusion, confusion, perversion, lethargy, inertia, extreme nature and behavior, carelessness, disregard for norms and rules, apathy, etc. Together, the three gunas determine the nature of our actions, decisions, intentions, behavior, conduct, and essential nature.

The Hindu caste system was designed to categorize people based on these criteria so that they can collectively work for their welfare and that of others, serving God and His creation in the process. This concept is subtly presented in the seventeenth chapter of the

Bhagavadgita, which proclaims that faith is closely linked to a person's essential nature. As a person is, so is the faith and resolve of that person. Righteous people worship the righteous God, the upholder of Dharma, and engage in righteous actions, unlike the unrighteous ones who engage in sinful actions, worship inferior gods, and criticize or question the very existence of God. Each person is made up of faith only, which arises from the triple gunas that are present in him. Thus, a person and his faith can be sattvic, rajasic, and tamasic, or a combination of all these. One can imagine in how many ways essential nature, faith, and resolve can arise in people from the permutations and combinations of the three gunas. These gunas determine not only the nature of their faith but also which gods or methods or paths they choose to practice it. They also determine which material and spiritual goals they may pursue.

Based on the duties assigned to each Varna, we may distinguish four ways in which human beings can perform their obligatory duties and serve God's eternal Dharma on earth. We may consider them the four paths to liberation. While the Vedic varnas are hereditary and a person's Varna and duties are determined by their birth and heredity, what is presented below is a brief account of how humans can serve God and participate in His creation according to their inherent nature rather than their genealogy, ancestry or family lineage. As the Upanishads, such as the Chandogya and Vajrasuchika Upanishads, suggest, a person's Varna is determined by his actions, conduct, knowledge, and character. One becomes a Brahmana by knowing and realizing Brahman. One becomes a Kshatriya by cultivating fearlessness and willingness to support and defend righteous causes with courage and resolve. In other words, one does not necessarily become a Brahmana, Kshatriya, Vaishya, or Shudra by birth but by one's nature and personality traits. This is emphasized in the Vedas itself. The Puranas also contain many illustrations. For example, Parasurama was born into a pious Brahmana family but was a Kshatriya by nature. Even Manusmriti supports the premise that a Brahmana earns respect and recognition by conduct, knowledge, and virtue, not by birth.

In the following discussion, we focus on these four paths that lead to peace, happiness, and liberation for those who pursue the four chief aims of human life and perform their obligatory duties as householders and upholders of God's eternal Dharma. It does not apply to those who renounce worldly life and pursue the path of renunciation to attain liberation as their ultimate aim. For them, the only prescribed path is the path of liberation (Moksha). Even in their case, their essential nature determines their methods and practices. Sattvic people choose sattvic methods, rajasic ones choose rajasic methods, and tamasic ones choose tamasic methods. The results and the time involved in achieving the goal may also vary. The four paths are presented below.

The path of Brahmanas

This is the chosen path of spiritually enlightened people such as God's worshippers and exclusive devotees, renunciants, intellectual people, spiritual masters, ascetics, scholars, philosophers, experts in various branches of knowledge, artists, yogis, etc., who are drawn to spirituality and engaged in studying, teaching, the propagation of Dharma, selfless actions, and helping and guiding others on the path of liberation. They represent the light of Brahman's pure intelligence and the best and the highest of humanity. They are dutiful, live righteously, and help others overcome suffering or find solutions to their problems. They live exemplary lives, serve as role models for others, and inspire others by setting standards of excellence in whatever they do. This is essentially the path of religious and spiritual people who believe in God and serve Him by serving others selflessly as an offering. This is essentially the path of Brahman that leads to supreme knowledge, fulfillment, contentment, peace, stability, and happiness.

The path of the Kshatriyas

This is the path of leaders, rulers, administrators, and authority figures with discernment and decision-making skills who take upon themselves the task of resolving problems and overcoming obstacles to reach their goals. With their knowledge, intelligence, courage, and wisdom, they open the minds of the ignorant and deluded and defend and protect those who depend upon them or look to them for help and support. Their authority may arise from their position in society, the support they receive from others, faith in themselves, or the knowledge and resources they possess. They are passionate, fearless, and brave and do not hesitate to speak their minds and stand for their beliefs, morals, values, and convictions. They take responsibility for their actions, persevere in reaching their goals, resolve conflicts, settle disputes, and use their wealth, strength, and power to promote peace and harmony or for the welfare of others, if necessary, by sacrificing their comforts and interests. This is essentially the path of enlightened leaders, teachers, and masters who lead and inspire others by personal example on the path of righteousness.

The path of the Vaishyas

This is the path of those engaged in generating and distributing wealth through agriculture, industry, trade, commerce, and related activities, suitable mainly for landowners, merchants, traders, businesspeople, money lenders, bankers, etc., who are engaged in various commercial and business activities. The Dharma Shastras stipulate that they must use that wealth not to fulfill their selfish desires but for the welfare of others and the world. They must live righteously, imbibe the knowledge of the scriptures, engage in sacrificial actions selflessly, give charity and gifts to others, and use their wealth for righteous causes. In the pursuit of Artha (wealth), they should not ignore the importance of Dharma and Moksha and should not resort to unjust methods to acquire wealth or indulge in evil passions wealth brings in its wake, such as pride, anger, lust, greed, envy, etc. Essentially, this is the path of riches on which people can become trapped unless they use discretion and discernment, cultivate detachment and renunciation, and stay away from evil influences.

The path of Shudras

This is the path of working people or commoners who rely mostly upon their physical strength and limited resources to survive in this world and support their families, serving and assisting others in their duties or reaching their goals. They may not be well-educated and may not have time or opportunity to study the scriptures, pursue higher education, acquire specialized skills, or indulge in intellectual pursuits. Yet, on this path, instead of blaming God or others or blaming themselves, they must strive hard to improve their karma and improve their condition. To that end, they must live virtuously and pursue their goals through hard work and exemplary character and conduct. They may not have much influence in society or wealth to support themselves or others, but they can win over people by helping them and earning their trust and support. Although they may not possess scriptural knowledge, knowledge of rites and rituals, or discernment to distinguish right from wrong, they can still practice simple devotion to God and earn his love and grace or find an escape from suffering. Thus, worshipping God in whatever they can, performing their obligatory duties within their means, living righteously without compromising their character and conduct, and exemplifying the virtue of 'simple living and high thinking,' they should pursue the four chief aims of human life.

All these paths are equal, neither superior nor inferior compared to each other. They all lead to the same goal: fulfillment and liberation. They all inflict pain and suffering upon all and spare no one if their karma stands in their way. One should, therefore, accept them and pursue them, knowing that suffering is a great teacher meant to teach us valuable lessons about ourselves and life in general and that if we pay attention, we can achieve progress through the paths we choose and reach perfection. In the past, these paths were meant for people born in the four castes. People had no choice but to follow the paths prescribed for them at birth, whether they suited them or not or whether it helped them achieve peace and fulfillment. Nowadays, Hindus have the freedom to follow their minds and hearts or their essential nature to choose their paths and professions or the lifestyles they want to lead. Circumstances, fate, and environmental factors still influence our decisions and choices. However, many of the restrictions associated with the caste system have disappeared. Hindus have the freedom to be what they want to be and how they want to live their lives. This is true, especially for a majority of them who live in the cities and are not suffocated by conventional discrimination. They can choose the path of Brahmana, Kshatriya,

Vaishya, or Shudra according to their convenience or wisdom and realize their true potential.

In Defense of the Caste System

The Hindu caste system is one of the most widely studied social systems in the world and one of the oldest social systems, if not the oldest. It still survives in a diluted form, retaining some of its original features. It still exerts considerable influence upon its followers in almost every aspect of their lives, from their personal and social relationships to their thinking, attitude, and behavior. I have presented my views on this topic several times in the past, sometimes critically, and examined it from various perspectives, suggesting that it would be better if we discontinue the caste divisions that exist in Hinduism to resolve the disunity and discrimination that arise from them and ensure its continuity. However, I am aware that by suggesting it, I was asking for the impossible because the roots of Hinduism are entrenched in the idea of Dharma, which primarily means obligatory duties that humans are supposed to perform on earth to keep their promise to God and play their dutiful role in His creation. Without fulfilling that promise and performing those duties, there is no Hinduism or Sanatana Dharma, so to speak. While working on this subject, it occurred to me that previously, while thinking and writing on this subject, I might have missed an important point about the inseparable connection of the caste system with the four phases of human life, which are identified and highlighted in the Varnashrama Dharma.

I want to cover that aspect in this chapter. I still believe the caste system negatively impacts Hinduism's unity and continuity, and at some point, Hindus must unite and set it aside to move on to the next century. However, the caste system had some positive features, which were somehow lost or ignored as Hinduism passed through many phases of reform and change. My conviction is that the caste system was introduced with many good intentions, but as has happened with many other systems, ideas, and inventions, it produced many unintended consequences. Given the human propensity to follow the path of the least resistance, the caste system was meant to establish order and regularity in society and establish specific laws and codes of conduct to which people could adhere according to their professions, occupations, or duties with which they were entrusted. It pointed them to certain ideals and a particular way of life, with God in the backdrop, by following which they could lead a balanced and holistic life and achieve fulfillment by pursuing their material and spiritual goals. It is a different matter that this ideal was lost as the system became stratified due to circumstances and gave scope to many abuses. In the following paragraphs I want to elaborate upon this premise.

Castes were meant to ensure obligatory duties

As a teacher, you know what happens if a teacher leaves his classroom and asks his students to maintain calm in his absence and not cause any disturbance. Most likely, when he returns, he will find them disregarding his instructions and doing whatever they normally do when a teacher is not present. Human nature is such that it yearns for freedom and is hardly amenable to discipline, order, and control. What force can then ensure order and regularity among people or that they will maintain discipline and decorum or follow proper norms, code of conduct, and social and ethical behavior without compromising their freedom? What can make them live responsibly and dutifully and engage in tasks that are not immediately rewarding but contribute to the welfare of all? A ruler has to perform many unpleasant tasks. In times of war, he must lead his army on the battlefield and ensure that his soldiers fight for him and protect him, putting themselves and their lives at risk. He must also punish those who disobey his laws or engage in criminal conduct. At the same time, he should become a tyrant and oppress people. A priest has to engage in exemplary conduct and spend his time in ritual and spiritual activities. Through his actions and conduct, he must set an example for others to follow. At the same time, he must ensure that his family enjoys basic comforts and that his children follow his footsteps and become guardians of the Dharma. Those who engage in the pursuit of wealth should ensure that their actions do not cause pain and suffering to others, and while they may engage in trade and commerce for profit or gain, they must also think of the welfare of others and be willing to share their wealth with them. Society also requires workers who rely solely on their physical strength to perform routine but difficult, low-paying, and boring or unpleasant jobs. They need motivation and some deterrence to stay in their comfort zones without disrupting the progress of society or creating chaos. How can you make soldiers go to war zones and fight terrible wars, knowing well that their chances of returning to their families are almost none to zero, or make people toil in the fields or factories all day long for meager wages without feeling envy or anger, while those who amassed great wealth and power live in luxury and enjoy their lives?

The Vedic seers, in their wisdom, must have foreseen these possibilities when they conceived the caste system. Their aim was to mitigate friction among diverse groups with varying interests and unite them under a common purpose, fostering social harmony, fraternity, and unity. They delineated four classes: Brahmanas, Kshatriyas, Vaishyas, and Shudras, and assigned specific duties and responsibilities to each class, all of which they traced back to divine will. This divine sanction lent their assignments a sense of validity, inviolability, and divine approval. The system was designed to ensure that individuals adhered to their duties and lived responsibly, thereby allowing life to progress normally, peace and harmony to prevail, and God's eternal Dharma to continue without major disruptions.

The caste system prescribed the highest standards of living for the Brahmans. The law books ordained that they should lead exemplary lives, observe the highest standards of purity, discipline, virtue, and morality, study the scriptures, and propagate Dharma by teaching and performing daily and occasional sacrifices according to the injunctions of the Vedas. They suggested that the Kshatriyas must assist their kings, defend them in times of war, and help them establish peace and prosperity on earth in peaceful times. The kings were supposed to be guardians of Dharma, avoid tyranny, vices, and evil passions, and take care of their subjects with love and compassion. Although the kings enjoyed power and protection, their lives were uncertain as they had numerous internal and external enemies. The warriors also lived uncertain lives since wars were frequent, and they did not know when they would lose their lives. Selukus, the Greek ambassador in the court of Chandragupta Maurya, noted that the emperor lived in utter fear for his life and never slept in the same room for two consecutive days. He also kept women soldiers to guard him since he could not trust anyone. It shows how fear and uncertainty dogged the ancient rulers and kept them confined to the inner circle of their friends and well-wishers. The Vaishyas were entrusted with the duty of accumulating wealth through agriculture, cattle-rearing, business, trade, and commerce. At the same time, the law books prescribed rules for them to ensure that they would not live selfishly or amass wealth at the expense of others. They were supposed to serve the other three classes by sharing their wealth with them and participating in religious and spiritual activities to promote and uphold Dharma. They were also made to depend upon them so that they would not lose sight of the importance of their social, economic, and moral responsibilities. Each of these three classes also had the obligatory duty to study the Vedas so that they knew their duties and responsibilities and lived righteously and responsibly.

Farmers, cattle herders, artisans, and unskilled workers constituted the fourth class, the Shudras. As the scriptures suggest, although they were denied Vedic education and relegated to a lower position in the social hierarchy, at times, they enjoyed the same status as the Vaishyas, owned lands and businesses, and interacted freely with others. They were barred from studying the scriptures because they wanted them to perform their duties and practice Dharma by following the instructions of the other three and executing their orders. If the other three lived responsibly and followed the injunctions of the Vedas and the Dharma Shastras, the working people would be well-protected, and no harm would come to them. While this was the theoretical reason for precluding them from the study of the Vedas and other scripture or from acquiring the right knowledge to achieve liberation, in practice that ideal was never uniformly practiced. As a result, the working classes suffered from disabilities, oppression, discrimination, and harsh living conditions. The caste system is a good example of how noble intentions can lead to unintended consequences due to the propensity of humans to succumb to their base nature and live selfishly.

In practice, the caste system also failed to resolve all group conflicts or ensure order regularity. It failed to take care of the outlier groups who either did not join the Vedic community or preferred to remain independent. Vedic people labeled them as outcastes (Chandalas), whom some scholars consider as the fifth class (panchama Varna). Their condition was truly deplorable, as they were treated with contempt as untouchables and were not allowed to socially interact or live within the proximity of these four groups. Unlike in other religions, little or no effort was made by the enlightened teachers of the upper castes to reform them, civilize them, teach them hygiene and self-care, or improve their living conditions so that they could be assimilated into society and the stigma associated with them could be removed. This is one major failure of the caste system. The upper castes enjoyed the privileges conferred upon them by the scriptures and the social system they proposed but failed to take care of their social and moral responsibilities, ignoring the fundamental truth enshrined in the Vedas that the Supreme Brahman resides in all as their very Self and all are equal and part of God's universal family.

Barring this failure, the system fulfilled much of its intended purpose. It helped the diverse traditions and sects of Hinduism survive difficult times, serving as a glue and keeping caste unity and cohesion intact despite the fact that they lacked centralized leadership or political power to defend themselves. The law books reinforced the beliefs associated with the caste system and its inseparable connection with God and His eternal duties, which humans are supposed to uphold as their own to ensure the progress, order, and continuity of the world. Each caste not only enjoyed certain privileges but also suffered from certain disabilities. Their privileges entailed observance of higher standards of morality, complex duties, and greater responsibilities. If they enjoyed better rewards, they also suffered from stricter and severe punishments and social ignominy for their moral and ethical transgressions. If Brahmanas enjoyed social privileges and higher status, they were also subject to stricter standards of morality and public scrutiny. In contrast, the lower castes were spared from similar expectations and stricter punishments unless they engaged in serious crimes.

Thus, the caste system was originally meant to establish a social order based on the division of work or duties and ensure social and economic justice and opportunities for various social groups according to their relative importance and contribution to society and the world. It guaranteed some degree of balance and orderly progression of society. It ensured a social order in which each caste was obligated to perform certain pleasant and unpleasant tasks that were essential for the overall welfare of the world and bear with advantages and disadvantages arising from that arrangement.

The present-day world is a good example of how any system can fall apart and lead to many negative consequences if people forget its original intent and purpose. The caste system still exists, although much of the rigidity associated with it in the past regarding occupations, duties, and responsibilities does not exist anymore. People can choose their occupations according to their knowledge, qualifications, circumstances, opportunities, and inclinations. The Indian army recruits people from all castes. Many Hindu temples employ priests and administrators from various social backgrounds. The same is the case with trade and commerce, the finance sector, government jobs, industrial and manufacturing sectors, healthcare, medicine, and so on. There are no restrictions since the Indian constitution prohibits discrimination explicitly. While this has a positive impact on people of all sections, on the downside, one can see a gradual decline in people's commitment to Dharma (their obligatory duties) and virtuous conduct.

Castes inculcated order and discipline

The hereditary caste system led to many social evils. But in itself, it does not validate that it is a flawed system. It aimed to establish and promote a certain way of life for each caste so that they perform their duties and fulfill their obligations. From the perspective of Varnashrama Dharma also, we can see that it offered a blueprint of life for each to follow without supervision. Imagine what would have happened if human beings had to decide arbitrarily the caste of each person after they were born. It would have led to a lot of confusion, conflicts and social chaos. The hereditary caste system precluded such possibilities and ensured that everyone followed the same laws and adhered to the order in which they found themselves. The karma doctrine justified it and helped it gain widespread acceptance. It pointed to the possibility that each embodied soul may take birth as a Brahmana, Kshatriya, Vaisya, or Shudra, according to their previous actions and accumulated karma. Actions determine the birth and destiny of each person and no external agency can be blamed for the suffering people go through. The Bhagavadgita confirms this argument.

An Upanishadic Perspective on Varna

Vajrasuchi means a sharp point, hard as a diamond and powerful like a thunderbolt. The name Vajrasuchika Upanishad (also spelled Vajrasucika) is a direct reference to its pointed attack against the caste system of Hinduism. It vehemently challenges the traditional and orthodox views about the caste system and the superiority of upper castes based purely on their birth, heredity, or ancestry or the argument that one attains Brahmanahood (Brahmanatvam) just by birth. True to its name, the Upanishad, with its decisive and sharp knowledge, aims to pierce through the delusion of ignorant people and open their eyes to the importance of seeking Brahman for liberation rather than taking pride in their birth, caste, or family status. In the very first verse, the Upanishad declares that its knowledge intends to dispel ignorance, condemn the ignorant, and elevate those who possess discernment. From this perspective, Vajrasuchi means the knowledge that leads to an unwavering and pointed mind and sharp intellect (shisha prajna).

The authorship

Traditionally, the Vajrasuchika Upanishad has been associated with the Samaveda. This could have a subsequent development, probably in the post-Buddhist era, since, according to some, it betrays Buddhist influence. Hence, the authorship of the text is attributed by some to Buddhist scholars, Asvaghosha or Dharmakirit, who were originally Brahmanas by birth and caste before they converted to Buddhism. A Buddhist text named Vajrasuci, which was said to have been translated in the 10th century CE by Fahien, the Chinese traveler to India, adds some credibility to this theory.

However, based on its criticism of the hereditary caste system or its characterization of a true Brahmana does not invalidate its roots in Vedism. Its views about the true Brahmana are also found in the law books. Hence, its essential philosophy is still rooted in Hinduism, and the beliefs it upholds are enshrined in the Vedas. It regards Brahman as the highest, supreme reality and the knowledge of Brahman as the means to liberation, which are the themes of all the

Upanishads. This aligns it more with Hinduism than Buddhism, which holds that the whole existence is characterized by impermanence, and therefore, neither an eternal Self nor an eternal Brahman can exist or be attainable.

Although the caste system defined and laid down the rules for Hinduism's social structure and defined the roles, responsibilities, and duties of each according to their castes, the system drew criticism from many quarters from within and outside Hinduism. Many ascetic traditions, sects like Shaivism, and other religions criticized its practice and its inherent flaws. The arguments put forward in the Upanishad closely resemble those of many saints and seers who opposed the caste system and its discriminatory practices. Even Manusmriti agrees with the arguments of Vajrasuchika Upanishad stating that one becomes a true Brahmana by knowledge and virtuous conduct, not by birth.

Indeed, in many respects, the Upanishad agrees with the views of Virashaivism, whose founder, Basavanana (12th century AD), was well known for his passionate opposition to the caste system. Shankaracharya also opposed caste discrimination and regarded all human beings as the embodiment of Brahman. Hence, some believe he may have composed the Upanishad. Probably, it represents the teachings of an ancient school with roots in Shaivism or Buddhism and might have found its way into Vedism through its inclusion as an Upanishad of the Samaveda. The approach of the Upanishad is simple. It raises the fundamental question, how do we know that someone is a Brahmana, and proceeds to refute every conventional answer. The following is a summary of the Upanishad.

What makes one a Brahmana?

The Upanishad dwells upon the meaning, significance, and purpose of a Brahmana. It begins with the inquiry about who a Brahmana is and what distinguishes him from others. Can he be distinguished by his body, caste, relationship with his family or other Brahmanas, knowledge of the Vedas, or obligatory duties? It then goes on to establish that none of them truly qualify him or distinguish him as a Brahmana. A person does not become a Brahmana merely because of his physical body, caste, birth, knowledge, actions, or religious duties because they are subject to impurities, change, and destruction. The same individual Self transmigrates into different bodies in different lives and dwells in them. Therefore, no one becomes a Brahmana because of the Self in him. His body is also not exceptional and does not distinguish him as a Brahmana because, like all other bodies, it is made up of the five elements only and, like them, it is subject to death and decay. We cannot also say his caste makes him a Brahmana because many seers and sages were not born into a Brahman caste or community (jati). Yet, they lived exemplary lives, became true knowers of Brahman, and attained Him. Also, he cannot be distinguished by knowledge alone since knowledge is not exclusive to a Brahmana or the Brahmana caste. Lastly, he does not become a Brahman by his obligatory duties since Kshatriyas and Vaishyas also perform similar duties, host sacrificial ceremonies to make offerings to gods and give gifts.

The Upanishad then goes on to answer who qualifies to be a true Brahmana. It states that a Brahmana perceives the Self without the duality of subject and object. The distinction of caste, traits, or actions is immaterial for him. He transcends such worldly considerations and remains indifferent to them, establishing himself in sameness. He stands out as the auspicious one who is free from evils, imperfections, and impurities and possesses knowledge, truth, bliss infinity. In short, he represents and reflects the eternal Self as his essential nature and dissolves his identity in it. Thereby, he becomes one with the eternal Self. He becomes self-existent, self-knowing, and without egoism and willfulness as the indweller and supporter of all.

Thus, the Upanishad declares that a person attains liberation and becomes a true Brahmana because of his effort and qualities, not because he is born in a family of Brahmanas, has the knowledge of the Vedas and sacrificial ceremonies, or belongs to the caste or community of Brahmanas. A true Brahmana attains self-realization by cleansing his mind and body and dissolving his limited, egoistic identity and selfish desires, attachments, and willful intentions in Brahman. Neither the elevation nor transformation of the subtle body leads him to that exalted status. Neither his intelligence, mental agility, nor the physical beauty of his color and form gives him a unique identity. What distinguishes as a true Brahmana is his realization of the highest truth.

The Vajrasuchika Upanishad is unique among all the Upanishads for the sweeping message it delivers against the conventional beliefs and practices of the caste system and the discrimination of people based on their birth and caste. Based on the same arguments, we can say that even women qualify as Brahmanas if they possess the knowledge of Brahman and attain oneness with Him, irrespective of to whom they are born or to which caste they belong. It cautions people not to take pride in their castes or family status but focus on their spiritual development to qualify as true Brahmanas. One attains Brahmanahood by spiritual effort, purity, and the realization of oneness with Brahman, but not by birth, caste, or any other external considerations. It exemplifies the principle of sameness and fairness, accepts all beings as equals as Brahman's manifestations, and gives hope to all people to work for their salvation, irrespective of their social, economic, or caste backgrounds. Indeed, Vajrasuchika Upanishad was a bold attempt in the past to question the justification of the caste system and the injustices and discrimination it approved and sanctioned for a long time, deriving its authority from the law books.

Reforming the Caste System

Hinduism teaches universal brotherhood. It recognizes all existence as the sacred manifestation of God and all beings, including animals, as the embodiment of God Himself. Yet, many Hindus, including the most educated ones and those who live abroad, habitually practice the caste system, or the Varna system, as it was originally known. Their words and public actions may not betray their caste prejudices, but their friendships, family and social relationships, and group affiliations betray their caste prejudices. A keen observer of human behavior will instantly notice how pervasive the influence of castes is upon the thinking, actions, and group dynamics of a large section of Hindus. Its influence can be seen in almost every aspect of life, in politics, sports, and almost every profession and institution. It is pervasive in many schools, colleges, universities, and other educational institutions. Many teachers and students alike align themselves with their respective castes and indulge in group politics.

Undoubtedly, the caste system is one of the chief vulnerabilities of Hinduism, if not the most debilitating. In terms of its disruptive influence on the foundation and preservation of Hinduism and the unity and integrity of its community, the caste system is perhaps the worst of all problems plaguing it. It disrupts the unity of the community, divides them into groups and subgroups, and puts them against one another. It weakens their resolve to stand united against common causes and the threat of conversions, letting vested interests take advantage of their disunity and keep them divided and distracted. It perpetuates economic and social disparities, widens the gap between the haves and have-nots, limits opportunities for disadvantaged groups to progress in life, and favors privileged and influential groups.

In theory, the caste system was meant to facilitate the division of labor, duties, and responsibilities necessary to ensure the order and regularity of society. However, in practice, it became unjust, as the hereditary caste system promoted inequalities and forced a large number of people to serve the privileged castes and remain subservient. It divided the people and kept a majority of them from participating in important social, economic, and political events, thereby creating scope for the invaders from the outside to defeat the native kings and rule the country for a long time. Even today, if Indian society is largely divided and in disarray, it is because the caste system still rules the minds of people. We may even trace many social evils like the dowry system, conversions, and gender bias to castes and caste-based discrimination.

The caste system, in its present form, is a threat to the stability, integrity, and future of Hinduism. It has the potential to disrupt the continuity and foundation of the religion and diminish its popularity, which is a matter of serious concern. The system has historically driven many to desperation, leading them to convert to other religions. Even Brahmanas, who traditionally upheld the caste system, have converted to Buddhism and Jainism either because they were dissatisfied with the social inequalities and injustices or because they found merit in those faiths. This exodus from Hinduism has occurred consistently many times in history, from ancient times to the present day, and continues to be a significant problem and source of conversions.

Indian constitution abolished untouchability and its practice in any form [15]. It states that enforcement of any disability arising out of it is a punishable offense under the law. The Untouchability (Offenses) Act 1955 further ended the practice. It explicitly states the offenses that fall under the act, such as "barring people from entering a public place, temple, or place of worship; denying a person access to sacred water bodies, wells, etc.; and stopping a person from using a dharamshala (charitable inn), restaurant, shop, hotel, hospital, public conveyance, educational institution, and any place of public entertainment." It also includes the denial of the usage of roads, rivers, riverbanks, cremation grounds, wells, etc., and offenses such as enforcing professional, trade, or occupational disabilities. However, the Constitution of India does not define untouchability. The courts clarified it and set precedence, stating that the word should be understood in the context of "how it had developed historically in the country." In 1980, the Supreme Court of India held that State governments had the responsibility to ensure that no one was discriminated against.

Current status

Although untouchability has been legally and constitutionally abolished, caste-related discriminatory practices and inequalities continue to persist in some parts of India. The influence of the caste system remains strong, manifesting in various forms, both in practice and at psychological levels. Caste identities, the social stigma historically associated with certain castes, and their discrimination based on such factors still persist. Some of these problems may remain concealed in public but often surface in social media posts and private gatherings, serving as a reminder that the embers of the past excesses are still alive and can reignite. The prevalence of caste-related prejudices and divisions within Hindu society is unmistakable, as we will explore in this chapter.

1. Inter-caste marriages are not approved or accepted in many Hindu families, especially those of higher castes. The resistance is greater if the bride belongs to a higher caste and the groom comes from a lower caste. They often provoke honor killings and violence against couples who marry against the wishes of their parents and elders.

2. Many castes have organizations and associations to protect their community interests or their members' welfare or lobby for their group interests with decision-making authorities. They play an important role in reinforcing caste identities, social distinctions, and economic privileges. They also wield considerable influence and dabble in local and national politics, using their collective strength and resources to mobilize voters from their communities and help their candidates who may also be from the same caste. While these associations fulfill the basic human need for group identity and belonging, promote group cohesion, provide moral or financial support to their needy members, and participate in several philanthropic and welfare activities not only for their communities but also for others, they also pose a problem to the Hindu community in general and add another layer of complexity to the system if they indulge in casteism and discrimination.

3. Many Indians resent the government's reservation policy and the justification for continuing it when the problem of poverty and many social and economic disabilities is universal and not confined to certain groups or castes. Some castes and non-Hindu groups insist on being recognized as backward castes or included in the list of Scheduled castes and tribes so that they can avail themselves of the government's benefits. Instead of addressing these issues and reforming the reservation policy, successive governments and political groups keep aggravating the problem by offering piecemeal solutions or promising more reservations for certain categories of people based on other criteria.

4. Caste conflicts often escalate into violence and unrest, particularly in educational institutions where students form groups based on their castes, often with the support of teaching faculties and outside groups. This problem also permeates workplaces, influencing matters of recruitment, wage increases, and promotions. Scheduled caste and tribe unions and organizations leverage their protected status to extract concessions, often resorting to false complaints of discrimination and criminal charges as a pressure tactic. These instances underscore the pervasive nature of caste-based discrimination in Indian society.

The country's democracy, which is the largest in the world and hugely successful, is also not free from the influence of castes. One may even call it a castocracy. Especially during elections, caste distinctions come to the fore when people vote for leaders who are chosen on caste lines and who flaunt their caste affiliations openly to ensure their electoral chances. The Indian political parties formulate their strategies to keep their voter bases along caste lines. The success of each party depends upon how many influential and wealthy leaders they secure from each caste. The government itself reserves a certain number of seats for scheduled castes and tribes. Thus, the very democratic process reinforces and brings to the fore caste divisions and prejudices with each cycle of elections and keeps the problem alive. This is even more pronounced in local government elections, where each election rekindles past rivalries, and group conflicts keep the problem alive.

5. Caste-based discrimination is practiced in many Hindu temples, especially in rural areas. Most temples, including the popular ones managed by government officials, do not recruit people other than Brahmanas for priestly duties. In some villages, lower castes are not allowed to enter temples despite the promulgation of the Untouchability Act, which explicitly prohibits it. Brahmanas continue to be the main choices for priestly jobs in major Hindu temples, partly because they are more qualified and dedicate themselves to the profession and partly because no noticeable effort has been made to encourage people from other castes to study the Vedas and undertake priestly duties. Shaivism, which has been traditionally opposed to caste discrimination, is an exception.

6. Discrimination against the lower castes continues in several places, and the local police often do not register cases reported by them against the offenders or try to silence them without due process. In many villages, they are not allowed to draw drinking water from the wells used by the higher castes or use the same facilities to cremate their dead. Due to caste prejudices, they continue to be the main choice for low-paying and menial jobs, which the higher castes are averse to performing. Many also dislike the idea of working under bosses belonging to lower castes or taking instructions from them. The prejudice is even more pronounced in the case of women who are subject to sexual harassment, violence, abuse, and exploitation.

7. Upper-caste families enjoy many social and economic advantages compared to lower castes, even if they belong to the same economic or financial category. This is especially true in rural communities where old cultural values still persist and exert their influence. Indians who visit foreign countries or migrate to them often complain about how the native people of those countries treat them because of their looks, accents, nationality, ethnicity, behavior, and social or cultural norms. Such discrimination indeed exists, although in most cases, it is not overly expressed. However, they should remember that many people in India also face discrimination because of their caste, color, appearance, language, accent, ethnicity, and faith. Skin color is also an important criterion in the selection of marriage partners. Indian films exemplify it by promoting fair-

skinned actors or putting heavy makeup on those who are dark-skinned to make them look fairer and agreeable to the audience.

8. The elites are also not free from its pervasive influence. Countless Hindu scholars, business leaders, and others with good educational qualifications, especially those with an orthodox mindset, justify the Hindu caste system, quoting references from scriptures, ignoring the possibility that they could be convenient interpolations of ancient scholars to justify and perpetuate in the name of God and religion and ensure their dominance and social and economic advantage.

What can we do about it?

The caste system might have served its purpose in ancient times. However, it does not fit into the values and principles of modern times, such as democracy, fundamental rights, individual freedom, equality, and non-discrimination. It does not uphold the values of modern Hinduism either, such as tolerance or universal brotherhood. It does not validate the concept that all life is the sacred expression of the creative forces of the universe, and they do not purposely or consciously discriminate against anyone. Hindu scriptures affirm that God, the Creator, is indifferent and looks upon everything equally. Therefore, those who wish to see Hinduism progress into the future or next century should not rationalize caste inequalities or discrimination of certain classes simply because of their birth or social background. If Hinduism has to remain credible and acceptable to a wider section of the global population, it must be willing to accommodate people of all nations, races, and backgrounds.

Those who rationalize the caste system by quoting the Purushasukta or the verses from the Bhagavadgita ignore the fact that they contradict the very core values and basic tenets of Hinduism emphasized in the same texts. The caste system needs an overhaul, not through the enforcement of any authority, but by a gradual change in the attitudes of Hindus themselves in the larger interests of their faith rather than their castes. It will help if they admit students from the lower castes into religious studies, including the study of the Vedas and other scriptures, and become teachers to educate others or serve as priests in the local temples. In Christianity, the clergy and missionaries are recruited from all sections of society if they are inclined to serve God and possess good character.

The caste system is Hinduism's chief weakness. It divides people into social groups, creates conflicts, and keeps them apart. If it is allowed to prevail in its current form, it would cause greater damage to Hinduism than we can imagine and impede its progress. Those who pay attention to the social and caste dynamics of Hinduism must have already seen its negative impact. Because of it, Hinduism has already lost millions of its followers to other religions, as people who felt alienated or discriminated against left it to become atheists or join other religions where they are treated with dignity and respect and allowed to feel good about themselves. Texts such as Manusmriti cannot be followed in the present-day world. It is time we consign them to the dustbins of history and move forward to establish an egalitarian society in which all members are treated equally as part of one divine family. If people develop compassion and understanding, many problems associated with the caste system will gradually disappear.

As we have discussed before, caste prejudices still exist in many parts of India, where lower castes are subjected to many disabilities and discrimination. In the worst-case scenarios, they are still not allowed to enter temples to offer prayers or draw water from the wells where upper castes live. As a result, many villages in the country, especially in the south, now have predominantly converted populations, though in theory, they may bear Hindu names and are regarded in the census as Hindus, more pastors than priests, and more churches than temples. One may blame the missionaries for the conversions, but the fact is the whole community is responsible for this. It will not happen with that frequency if people belonging to the downtrodden sections feel included and are treated well.

As Hindus, we take pride in Hinduism's historicity and proudly proclaim it as an eternal religion (Sanatana Dharma) of peace, tolerance, spirituality, and enlightenment. We ignore the fact that such tolerance should be extended to all community members first. The caste system, as such, is not the problem since the diversity of human populations is a fact, and some kind of social order is necessary to provide for their diverse skills, talents, and temperaments. Caste-based discrimination is the problem. Hindus can have an equitable caste system that accommodates all classes and types of people and treats them equally as beings with divine souls, recognizing their right to live with dignity and respect. To appreciate the value of human birth and the equality of all beings, which is actually the foremost ideal of Hinduism, we do not have to look far. Within Hinduism itself, we have some sects, traditions, and doctrines that oppose the caste system and preach social equality and universal brotherhood. Many saints and seers in the past fought against the caste system. They preached universal love, tolerance, sameness, and compassion towards everyone.

In this regard, Shaivism, one of the oldest Hindu sectarian traditions, sets an example by opposing the caste system and caste-based discrimination. From the earliest times, the followers of the sect preached against empty ritualism, pretentious worship, and unjust treatment of the lower castes and outcastes. They emphasized spiritual purity, social equality, and the right to worship God by all according to their faith, nature, and inclination, offering them different paths and methods to pursue liberation. Lord Shiva Himself embodies and represents the opposites of human nature. The sect recommends both conventional and unconventional methods of worship and spiritual practice. The Shiva temples are open to everyone. Anyone can walk into them and offer prayers or offerings of water, milk, etc., with or without the mediation of priests. The practice continues even today. The priests in the Shiva temples also hail from different social and caste backgrounds.

Hindus can take inspiration from the teachings and practices of Shaivism to reform the caste system and remove the flows for which it is known. They can improve it by returning to its original form where people had the freedom to choose their occupations irrespective of their castes and where they were not subjected to discrimination but valued for their contribution to the welfare of all. Those who serve others are not inferior. They exemplify the ideal of sacrifice and the virtue of humility and egolessness. Therefore, people who are engaged in menial jobs deserve respect and recognition for their contribution to society. They may belong to any caste. Ideally, we must allow people to choose their occupations and live with dignity. Only then can we justify the caste system and not let it become a source of conflict, discrimination, and oppression.

Footnotes

1. Fahien mentioned that when the Chandalas entered a city or a street, they were required to strike a price of wood to warn others of their coming so that people moving in the streets would not be polluted by their contact, 31.

2. A twice-born man who knowingly eats mushrooms, a village pig, garlic, a village-cock, onions, or leeks will become an outcast. (5:14). A Brahmana who neither performs austerities nor studies the Veda, yet delights in accepting gifts, sinks with the (donor into hell), just as (he who attempts to cross over in) a boat made of stone (is submerged) in the water. (4.190), 34.

3. A Brahmana who takes a Sudra wife to his bed will (after death) sink into hell; if he begets a child by her, he will lose the rank of a Brahmana. (Manusmriti: Ch3:17), 34.

4. Let (the first part of) a Brahmana's name (denote something) auspicious, a Kshatriya's be connected with power, and a Vaisya's with wealth, but a Sudra's (express something) contemptible. (Manusmriti: Ch2:31), 36.

5. Manusmriti, Chapter 7:35, 36.

6. Manusmriti Chapter 7:14, 36.

7. It is said that those who spoke Dravidian languages probably lived in the Indus Valley and present-day Rajasthan before migrating eastward and southward due to climatic changes. They practiced some form of a caste system based on vocations that was later adopted by Vedic priests as a model for their social order as Vedic religion grew in complexity due to the integration of traditions such as Vaishnavism, Shaivism, and Tantrism. 40.

8. He is also considered the progenitor of the Andhras of the South. Today, they constitute the second or third-largest linguistic group in India. 39.

9. Prof K.P. Jayaswal, 44.

10. According to H.G. Rawlinson, caste is a Portuguese word meaning purity of race. 44.

11. The Satavahanas, who ruled in the early Christian era, patronized Brahmanism and contributed greatly to its revival in southern and central India. Their empire extended from the river Krishna in the south to Malwa and Kathiawar in the north and also included large parts of present-day Maharashtra and some parts of Gujarat and Orissa. 47.

12. The Purusha Sukta verse dealing with the creation of castes is

reproduced below. 66.

> *When they divided the Purusha, how many portions did they make?*
> *What do they call his mouth, his arms? What do they call his thighs and feet?*
> *The Brahman was his mouth, and of both his arms was the Rajanya made.*
> *His thigh became the Vaisya; from his feet, the Sudra was Produced.*

13. Bhagavadgita Ch 4:14, 67.

14. Bhagavadgita Ch 6:42, 67.

Cover Design: Jayaram V
Front cover background image: Adobe Express

www.ingramcontent.com/pod-product-compliance
Lightning Source LLC
Chambersburg PA
CBHW061809070526
44586CB00024B/2777